Table of Contents

The Hawaii Architectural Foundation is pleased to provide this book titled _The Renaissance of Honolulu - The Sustainable Rebirth Of An American City_ to inspire planners, architects, the design profession, the construction industry and government leaders around the world to build vibrant and sustainable communities.

Aloha,

HAWAII ARCHITECTURAL FOUNDATION

November, 2005

Magic Island at Ala Moana Park. After a century of unsustainable growth and development, Honolulu is now on a path to a sustainable future.

Forward

The Renaissance of Honolulu

"The Building of a Sustainable City"

"Do not dream of what other cities may have done ... develop your own individuality, be Hawaiian, be a more beautiful Honolulu"

A year after Oahu's county government was organized in 1905, a visiting urban planning expert offered advice on the development of Honolulu's park system. Charles Mulford Robinson was amazed at the natural splendor he encountered during his stay. "There is the chance," he observed, "to make this one of the most beautiful cities of the world—all one great park, with a city tucked in between."

In the years and decades that followed, Honolulu became widely regarded as one of the world's greatest cities. But while incomparable beauty and multicultural history set us apart, the city's growth reflected the challenges and changes of a dynamic century. Population growth, urbanization, the post-war economic boom, and tourism's rapid expansion hastened Honolulu's modernization, and transformed the City in many unsustainable ways.

Poor land use policy prompted urban sprawl, covering much of the island's open space and agricultural land with asphalt and subdivisions. Having separated people's homes from their places of work and school, freeways were needed for transportation, causing air pollution and urban run-off. Historic neighborhoods were forever changed as highway arterials held sway.

In short, our island home was rebuilt around the automobile. No longer were we a city built around people and the traditional neighborhood—we were a city controlled by the car.

Just as Honolulu's land-use policies were unsustainable, so too was her economic development. The last century saw the rise and fall of plantation agriculture and the emergence of tourism as king. We were quickly putting all of our economic eggs in one basket. Not surprisingly, visitors flocked to Honolulu to see the island's pristine environment and natural beauty, and to experience the unique island culture. Success for the tourism industry was measured by the number of visitors coming to the island each year.

But the model was not sustainable. The rapid growth of tourism began destroying the very things visitors were coming to see. Air pollution from the burgeoning automobile population and polluted streams and beaches from inadequate waste management systems diminished the visitor experience, as well as the quality of life for the island's residents. On top of the environmental deterioration, the cultural heritage that visitors were coming to experience was becoming less and less authentic with the crass commercialization of Waikiki.

We were losing our Hawaiian "sense of place," the very mainstay of our economy and the soul of our island community.

Without economic diversification, our island community became more vulnerable to events outside our control, such as perturbations in the Japanese economy or terrorist attacks halfway around the world.

With the growth of tourism came the growth of population. Visitors came to experience the island, liked what they saw and decided to stay. Honolulu was no longer a sleepy tropical Polynesian town, it was on its way to becoming the 12th largest city in the U.S.

Along with this population explosion came an explosion of waste. Valleys became landfills, and the volume of sewage quickly overwhelmed the capacity of the city's wastewater pipes and pumps to deal with the flow. Streams and beaches suffered.

Once again, growth was having its impact on paradise.

Honolulu's urban growth was damaging to more than its environment. It was also playing havoc with neighborhoods and communities. The great homogenization of Oahu had begun. Historic districts were gutted in the name of urban renewal. Good urban design principles were ignored in the rush for quick development, and many architectural treasures were lost forever.

Honolulu, now the most livable large city in the world, has become a model for rapidly urbanizing communities internationally.

The demand for housing drove suburban sprawl and turned more and more of the island's open space and precious agricultural land into cookie-cutter subdivisions, without trees, without context, without community. Restoring the lost sense of community has been the challenge of the past ten years.

This book chronicles Honolulu's path over the last century of change and details efforts in the last decade to rechart its path to a more sustainable future.

We know today that the energy we use, the transportation systems we develop, and the land use decisions we make are all vital in determining the course of Oahu's future, and in a broader context the viability of our planet as a whole.

We offer our city of Honolulu as a model for the rapidly urbanizing world. We are a model of mistakes that led to unsustainable outcomes to be sure, but we are also a model for how a city can be reborn with vision and community leadership to be a truly sustainable cosmopolitan city.

We offer this book as a tribute to the renaissance of the City and County of Honolulu on her 100th birthday. Published on the eve of our centennial anniversary, it reminds us of how far we've come and offers a shining hope for the future—a future firmly grounded on a strong and sustainable foundation.

Kahana Bay

Chapter 1

The Renaissance of Honolulu
The Sustainable Rebirth of an American City

The people of Honolulu are blessed to live in a land of great beauty and abundant natural resources, and we take seriously our responsibility as stewards of the environment. Concern for the environment is woven into the culture of our community, and is a reflection of the respect that native Hawaiians have always had for the land and ocean that sustain us.

Oahu was once a model for environmental sustainability. The island was settled more than a thousand years ago by Polynesian explorers who migrated across the Pacific in voyaging canoes. The early Hawaiians were deeply connected to the land and their natural surroundings.

They developed sophisticated agriculture and aquaculture practices within carefully tended watershed ecosystems known as ahupuaa—divisions of land that stretched from mountaintops to the reef systems along the ocean shore. The Hawaiians were seasoned mariners and cultivators of the land. They understood that natural resources were abundant, but not unlimited. They built complex systems of canals, trenches and fishponds and used water in highly efficient ways to grow taro and raise fish. They were the earliest proponents of sustainable practices.

In time, Honolulu became the Pacific gateway to America—a multicultural community where people of diverse ethnicities and backgrounds have lived in harmony for more than a century. In the late nineteenth and early twentieth centuries, workers from China, Japan, Korea, the Philippines and other countries came to the islands to work in commercial agricultural fields. As they labored side by side on sugar and pineapple plantations, they shared the languages, cultures and customs of their ancestors. The intermingling of their values with those of the native Hawaiians created a new social dynamic called the *aloha* spirit. This spirit embodies the life-affirming qualities of social harmony, tolerance, and respect for the natural environment— values important for a sustainable island community.

But with the spread of plantation agriculture followed by urbanization of the island and the explosive growth of tourism, the sustainable practices of the host Hawaiian culture were lost.

Unsustainable energy and transportation policies required the importation of fossil fuels for electricity and transportation. Poor land use practices caused suburban sprawl and wiped out agricultural land. Inadequate waste management practices polluted the land and water. Everywhere you looked, from tourism development to invasive species, from urban design to water policy, Honolulu's citizens were not living sustainably.

Over the last decade, we have attempted to set our city on a new sustainable path. To reverse decades of unsustainable development centered on the automobile, we established urban growth boundaries and redirected growth to the Ewa plain and the urban core. We developed "smart growth" policies that promote mixed use development where people can live, work and shop, without having to depend on the automobile.

To slow the suburban sprawl across central Oahu, historic neighborhoods such as Chinatown were revitalized and hundreds of new housing units were developed.

To further reduce dependence on cars, we expanded the bus system, making it the best in North America, and we developed the first phase of the Hybrid Electric Bus Rapid Transit System.

To make our economy more sustainable, we revitalized Waikiki and restored its Hawaiian "sense of place." Our visitor industry was diversified with the development of world-class athletic facilities, heralding a future of sports tourism.

Shoreline Park. Thousands of acres of new parks, public art, and tree-lined streets typify Honolulu's renaissance.

And eco-tourism and edu-tourism were furthered with the redevelopment of Hanauma Bay, the preservation of Waimea Valley and the restoration of historic districts such as Chinatown.

To protect the environment and provide for a population of almost a million people, cutting-edge technology was deployed to collect and treat sewage, recycle waste and generate energy.

And to enhance the quality of life for our island families, we added thousands of acres of parks, graced the city with public art and planted thousands of trees.

The beauty of this urban rebirth, this renaissance of Honolulu, is that it has been community led. The Vision Process, the empowerment of citizens through grassroots democracy, has been instrumental in redirecting the City and County of Honolulu on a new sustainable path reminiscence of its ancestral past.

Our hope is that the lessons we have learned along the way and the principles of urban sustainability we have implemented, will be of value to other cities around the world as they face similar challenges.

Urban Sprawl. Cities of the 21st century need to be designed sustainably, based on a new paradigm of "smart growth" that minimizes the need for automobiles and ends urban sprawl.

Chapter 2

The Challenge of Sustainability

It is finally dawning on those of us in the developed world that the prosperity we enjoy, our "high life" as it were, is based on false accounting.

One fifth of the world's population has been consuming 75 percent of the world's resources—voracious consumption as if there was no tomorrow. Well, tomorrow has arrived. Quite simply, we have been living in an unsustainable paradigm of consumption and waste generation. We have assumed that the earth's resources are limitless and as we consume, we don't account for the expenditure of this "natural capital." At the same time, we assume that the earth has the ability to absorb an infinite amount of waste resulting from our consumption, and therefore, we don't account for the external costs of our production and pollution.

For example, we don't debit the environmental ledger when an estuary is bulldozed for urban development. Nor do we add the cost of respiratory disease caused by the air pollution from manufacturing to the price of the products we consume.

Take a simple gallon of gasoline. If we were to account for all its true costs, we would have to pay much more than we are now paying at the pump. The "opportunity cost" of depleting this finite natural resource and not being able to use it again and again for such things as plastic, is never calculated. The damage to the environment from the extraction and transportation of crude oil, the greenhouse gas pollution from its refining, and the exorbitant cost in public health, acid rain, and global warming from oil combustion is never added to the cost of the gas--not to mention the billions of dollars in military expenditures to control areas of production.

Would we consume as much fossil fuel if we knew what it was really costing us? Probably not. False accounting has that effect.

So what does all this have to do with sustainable cities?

We have now reached a milestone in human civilization. The urban era is upon us. Half of the world's population now lives in cities, and in our Asia-Pacific region the rate of urbanization is staggering.

Our region today is home to 3.5 billion people. In the next 20 years, that population will grow to about 5 billion. Over that time, hundreds of millions of people will be moving to cities.

As they become urbanites they also become consumers—of cars, gas, TV, refrigerators, all of the commodities we have coveted. Can you blame them? Of course not, but a quick check of the math shows that something has to give. The 20 percent of the population that lives in the developed world is consuming 75 percent of the earth's resources, and the other 80 percent of the population that is developing and urbanizing wants to consume at the same rate.

There are not enough resources to support this increased consumption, and the global environment couldn't possibly withstand the impact.

Something has to change, and that something is how we build and manage our cities. Cities of the 21st century need to be sustainable, based on a new paradigm of conservation and reuse and abandoning the old ways of consumption and waste.

We need to institute honest bookkeeping and truly account for the environmental, social and cultural costs of our actions. We need to realize that when it comes to running cities, good environmental policy is good economic policy.

Once city governments start making strategic decisions based on accurate long-term cost-benefit analysis instead of the simplistic short-term thinking of the past, the world will change.

Diamond Head and Waikiki Beach, Circa 1900 (J.A. Gonsalves, Bishop Museum); Downtown Honolulu to Waikiki today.

It will be apparent that clean renewable energy is more affordable than burning coal for electrical production, and that public mass transit systems powered by electricity or fuel cells are more advantageous than building cities around fossil fuel powered automobiles.

It will be obvious that recycling wastewater and solid waste is more cost effective than polluting streams and aquifers with wastewater and leachate.

Honest accounting will encourage sustainable decisions. Building sustainable cities will change the world.

As a gateway between the East and the West, and as an urban island ecosystem, Honolulu has unique responsibilities and opportunities in this regard. Our responsibility is to be a model of sustainability for the Asia-Pacific region and provide our developing neighbors with guidance on how to avoid the failed paradigm of consumption and waste. Our opportunity is to be a model of sustainability and to export knowledge and technology to the rest of the region that needs it so desperately.

Ahupuaa. The ancient Hawaiians managed the land in ecological units – the ahupuaa, entire watersheds stretching from the mountain top to the outer edge of the reef.

Chapter 3

The Land

Malama Aina

Building a sustainable city starts with good land use policy. If you don't get land use right, all else fails as well. Land use drives infrastructure, determines transportation systems, influences energy policy, affects economic development and impacts quality of life in numerous ways. You have to get land use right, and on Oahu, we didn't.

This is especially surprising since the ancient Hawaiians had it right. They managed the land in ecological, geographic units … the ahupuaa, which are land divisions stretching from the mountain top to the outer edge of the reef. By managing the land in a sustainable way, they were able to effectively manage their watersheds, protect forest and wildlife resources and optimize agricultural production.

There is no need to romanticize ancient Hawaiian sustainability. They made some mistakes. They drove some species to extinction. But by and large, they were good sustainable stewards of the land, and we can learn a lot about sustainable land management from their example. They lived *malama aina*, they nurtured the land.

Plantation Land Use

With the westernization of the islands came the concept of land ownership and the division of lands into parcels that had no relevance to watersheds or ecological units. Concentration of land ownership accompanied the rise of plantation agriculture and massive environmental damage ensued. Clearing of native habitats, introduction of invasive species, topsoil runoff into reefs and estuary habitats, pollution of aquifers with agricultural chemicals. The environmental damage to the *aina* from the plantation era was immense.

The habitation patterns that plantation agriculture spawned, however, were far more sustainable. Plantation agriculture brought with it the rise of the plantation camp. These camps were built near the fields that workers tended, so there was no need for individual automobiles to get to work—you either walked or rode a short distance in the back of the plantation truck.

Plantation agriculture transformed Oahu, destroying the native habitat and altering habitation patterns. Pineapple pickers in Kunia, Circa 1959 (Hawaii State Archives). Pineapple was second only to the sugar industry, Circa 1900 (Hawaii State Archives).

Each camp had its own general store and school, so cars and highways weren't needed for shopping or getting the children to class in the morning. And in later years, most camps even had their own movie theater where, for a dollar, the whole family could see a new movie every night.

Perhaps the most important aspect of the plantation camp was its sense of community. People knew their neighbors, they took care of each other, they shared what they had—the bananas from the back yard or the *akule* fish caught the night before. No one ever returned an empty plate.

The camps were based on what we today would call "smart growth" sustainable principles. And while they need not be over idealized (they had their problems with infrastructure and sewage treatment), the camps had a sense of place and identity, a sense of community, something we have lost in today's world.

The Birth of Urban Sprawl

Honolulu's gravest mistakes in land use policy came about with the increase in population that accompanied the diversification of the economy into tourism.

The growing number of people working in non-agricultural jobs created pressure for housing. Large landowners were only too happy to set aside lands for new subdivisions, which were far more lucrative than sugar or "pine." And so the island's first bedroom communities were born.

Poor land use planning in the last half of the 20th century encouraged the suburbanization of Oahu's open space and prime agricultural land.

Unlike camp life, people now lived in one part of the island and had to commute to town to go to work in the mornings. Schools and shops were developed in regional centers that could only be reached by car. The automobile society was born.

With the advent of the post-war baby boom and the "jet age", more and more people came to the island, and more agricultural land was consistently converted to subdivisions, each further from town than the last. The evolution of this new automobile-driven land use policy had enormous implications for the island's environment and for the quality of life of residents.

The subdivisions that sprung up had no real sense of community. People spent lots of time commuting and less time at home. Their affiliations became job-based, not neighborhood-based. Neighbors remained strangers, always in the car, shopping, or commuting. The sense of community that had been so strong in the camp society was lost. Home was where you slept and little more.

The Death of Downtown

The subdivision culture also had profound impacts on Downtown Honolulu and older community commercial centers. Downtown small businesses couldn't compete with regional automobile-based shopping centers, and so they closed their doors. This was accompanied by an exodus of downtown residents as people left the dying urban center for the "good suburban life."

The result was downtown urban decay. Downtown Honolulu became a ghost town in the evenings, as it rolled up the sidewalks at 6:00 p.m. Chinatown at night—once vibrant—was abandoned to the shadier elements of society. It became a combat zone of strip clubs, drugs and prostitution.

The decay of the urban core was not a phenomenon unique to Honolulu. It occurred all across the country, as city after city was rebuilt around the automobile. The Federal prescription for healing this outbreak of urban blight was predictably ill-conceived. It was euphemistically called "urban renewal" and consisted of the wholesale demolition of historic town cores all over the nation.

Instead of realizing that the "sense of place" in old urban centers was a valuable asset to be protected and nurtured, historic buildings, architectural treasures and whole neighborhoods were razed for homogenized redevelopment.

Modern Honolulu was developed around the automobile. This poor planning destroyed neighborhoods, polluted the environment and created a dependency on imported fossil fuels for transportation. Top Left: Diamond Head, Circa 1950 (Hawaii State Archives).

26

The Car is King

Not surprisingly, urban renewal largely failed and suburban sprawl continued. Our island community was completely redesigned around the automobile. The car was king.

The impact of this phenomenon was far more profound than simply the death of downtown. Our whole world was restructured around the automobile. Enormous resources were devoted to larger and larger highways going further and further into the country. More and more time was spent commuting as "peak hour" stretched to eight hours a day. The environmental impacts of road development were significant: thousands of acres of valuable land forever committed to asphalt, air pollution from the combustion of millions of gallons of fossil fuels each year and the runoff of heavy metals and road wastes into our steams.

We had put cars before people. We had rebuilt our city around the automobile and in doing so had destroyed our neighborhoods, lost our sense of community, polluted our environment, and permanently altered our family life.

Regulating Land Use

The first effort at land use control was embodied in the State Land Use law. Hawaii Revised Statutes, Chapter 205, enacted in 1961, was designed to protect our agricultural lands from this onslaught of development.

This agricultural protection law and the accompanying Land Use Commission (LUC) were put in place before the City and County of Honolulu had any real land use planning infrastructure.

In a number of cases, this innovative new law protected valuable agricultural land from poorly conceived development, but within a short period of time, the LUC simply became a regulatory and political tool rather than a planning tool and its effectiveness was lost.

In 1978, the State Constitutional Convention attempted to deal with the problem by amending the State Constitution to growth control and protect agricultural lands. This effort too ran afoul of state political interests, and although these policies are the law of the land, they have not been implemented to this day.

With the 1970s and '80s came an explosion of land use regulations from the City and County of Honolulu. Although land use decision-making at the City Council was typically based on political expediency rather than planning criteria, the Development Plans, Land Use Ordinance, and Special Design District regulations often kept the worst of development proposals from reaching the floor.

Despite all these new regulations, planning for Oahu was still based on the automobile.

It wasn't until the City adopted the enlightened policy that future growth should be directed to the Primary Urban Center (PUC) and to a new second city in Kapolei that the battle against suburban sprawl was engaged. Finally, a policy was in place that could stop the sprawl across the agricultural lands of Central Oahu and concentrate development so that housing could be built where people worked and shopped.

Unfortunately, before the ink had dried on the new policy, City planners were instructed to interpret the Ewa "secondary urban center" to include major portions of Central Oahu.

Good politics and good planning aren't always synonymous, and in this case a potentially effective land use planning tool was redefined into uselessness.

Stopping Sprawl

The latest regulatory efforts to restructure land use policies to redevelop the city around people and neighborhoods instead of automobiles are the Sustainable Community Plans and the Smart Growth Design Code.

In the past, each area of the island had a Development Plan that laid out the development planned for that region. Since the City's new goal was to restrict suburban sprawl and redirect growth to the urban centers, the Development Plans for each part of the island, except downtown Honolulu and Ewa, were redone with exhaustive community input to become Sustainable Community Plans.

"Smart Growth" policies encourage the transformation of automobile-oriented communities into more livable neighborhoods.

For the first time, definitive Urban Growth Boundaries were established all over the island to stop sprawl and protect our open space and agricultural lands.

Obviously, more was needed to stop sprawl than urban growth boundaries. New approaches to zoning, transportation, and urban design had to be created to promote the development of livable communities, communities that were designed around people, not cars. The new approach, tagged the Sustainable Smart Growth Design Code, in many ways harkened back to some of the most successful elements of traditional European cities.

The Smart Growth concept encourages mixed-use development so that people can live near their work, shopping, schools and recreational facilities. It promotes communities that minimize the reliance on the automobile. Smart Growth enhances public transportation opportunities, provides mobility for people and reduces traffic. In early 2004, the City's Department of Planning and Permitting partnered with the Environmental Protection Agency (EPA), the University of Hawaii Sea Grant College, the Urban Land Institute, and major developers to reverse the expansion of urban sprawl. The goal was to provide a framework for creating communities and neighborhoods instead of "bedroom subdivisions."

The resulting series of workshops were attended by developers, government officials and members of the community. Together they reviewed and revised not just the upcoming development proposals, but regulations that help shape new development on Oahu from a Smart Growth perspective. As a result, new communities are being built on Oahu that put people first and foster the creation of walkable, livable neighborhoods.

Revitalizing Agriculture

High priced real estate and the highest paid agricultural workers in the world spelled the end of plantation agriculture in Hawaii. With the death of the plantation came tens of thousands of acres of fallow agricultural lands.

The City's goal is for much of that land to be put back into some form of agricultural production. While a handful of hardworking entrepreneurial farmers have been able to successfully grow diversified crops, vast tracts of land remain empty. One of the obstacles to diversified agriculture is the price of land. Since landowners have traditionally been able to get their land rezoned from agriculture to urban use, the price of agricultural land is set at a speculative, potentially up-zoned value instead of at a value that could be supported by an agricultural crop. The result: you can't afford to grow cucumbers on $90,000 per acre land.

The proposed 83,000 acres of agricultural land is a vital part of Honolulu's land use planning to keep the country, country and promote the growth of diversified agriculture.

The only way to bring the price of agricultural land down to its true agricultural value is to guarantee that prime agricultural land will never be up-zoned. A bill to do just that, to protect 83,000 acres of prime agricultural land on Oahu in perpetuity, languished in the City Council for over two years, never receiving a fair hearing. A new bill has recently passed the Planning Commission and gone to the City Council that would reopen this issue. A complementary bill to provide tax breaks for landowners who actually farm their land also met with resistance from members of the Council, but was successfully adopted into law.

It's clear, large land owners want to protect their ability to urbanize their agricultural land and maximize their profits. Understandably, they don't want to pay higher taxes or receive lower prices for the vacant land they are waiting to urbanize. It's also clear, however, that for our island to become truly sustainable, we need to increase our agricultural production and reduce our dependence on imported agricultural products that can be grown in our own backyard. Honolulu should not have to import most of the bananas it consumes. Even more, we need to maintain the green open space that agriculture provides in order to sustain our visitor industry and recharge our freshwater aquifers.

Agriculture is important to the future of the island for food, jobs, the environment and our quality of life. If some champions of agriculture don't emerge soon, we may be hearing its death knell on Oahu.

Affordable Housing

Housing presents Honolulu with the classic "growth control" conundrum. If we want to control growth on our island, as most people do and as our State Constitution mandates, then we need to control development. If you control development, you reduce the amount of housing that's being built. This limits population growth, but it also increases the price of Oahu housing. When any commodity is in short supply and enjoys a global market, as real estate does in Hawaii, its price goes up. The dilemma is that our sons and daughters cannot afford to compete in this global market for high priced Honolulu housing.

In the late 1980s, housing was the number one issue facing the island. Exacerbated by runaway Japanese speculation, skyrocketing prices put housing out of reach for the average Hawaii family. Earning between 80 percent and 120 percent of median income, and dubbed the Gap Group, the majority of Honolulu's families simply couldn't afford a home of their own.

To try to address the problem, City and State governments jumped in with aggressive building programs. The City's strategy was to attempt to solve several "sustainability" problems at one time.

First, our overarching goal was to provide affordable housing for Honolulu residents in all income levels, from the homeless to the Gap Group, from the elderly to those with special needs.

Second, we wanted our housing efforts to help in our battle against suburban sprawl. We wanted to revitalize the downtown core and make Downtown/Chinatown a vital, prosperous, residential and commercial district. At the same time, we wanted to provide impetus to our plan for a second city in Kapolei by developing residential communities in the Ewa Plain.

By and large these efforts were enormously successful. We coupled housing development in Chinatown with a complete revitalization of the historic district. Led by City architect and planner Ben Lee, the City's focus on urban design had begun.

Chinatown was transformed. Historic lighting, cultural signage and trees graced the streets. Granite pavers reminiscent of the ballast blocks from historic sailing ships repaved the sidewalks.

Almost a thousand rental units were built in Chinatown/Downtown, following strict architectural design parameters, which brought more people and economic vitality to the area.

Underground parking, police facilities, markets, parks and community centers were added. Chinatown was no longer a "combat zone," a decayed urban core of Honolulu. It was now a great place to live, work and shop.

The seedy core of downtown Honolulu has been revitalized with the Chinatown Gateway Plaza and Park.

Marin Tower provides new rental apartments for people moving back to the urban core, but reflects the architecture of historic Honolulu.

The City has restored the historic district of Chinatown – making it a great place to live, work, shop, dine and enjoy recreational opportunities.

39

(Top) Chinatown/Downtown before Harbor Village revitalized the waterfront at Honolulu Harbor. Area fronts Honolulu Harbor. To the left is Nuuanu Stream. (Bottom) View of Chinatown looking toward Diamond Head and downtown high-rises. In the foreground is Harbor Village fronting Nimitz Highway and Nuuanu Stream.

40

Harbor Village. Harbor Village is one of many old parking lots that the City has transformed into apartments and shops in its revitalization of Downtown Honolulu.

To meet the needs of those wanting an affordable single-family home, we directed our efforts to the Ewa Plain, our second focus for directed growth to reduce Central Oahu's suburban sprawl.

The project was West Loch Estates and it was unlike any project the City had ever undertaken. Situated on underutilized, degraded land formerly owned by Oahu Sugar Company, West Loch Estates, was designed to be an integrated community of affordable and market homes, elderly housing and townhouses, all surrounding a central golf course and shoreline park.

Once again, good urban design and architectural detail were paramount. The resulting community with its tree-lined streets, moss rock walls, and lovely green belts was an enormous success.

With single-family affordable homes starting under $100,000, the project paid for itself. West Loch demonstrated that the price of housing in Hawaii is not based on the cost to produce the housing or by the cost of the land. The price of housing on Oahu is determined by market demand.

To deal with the problem of global competition for our housing, the City placed restrictions on the sale of the affordable homes. Purchasers had to be local residents and meet strict income criteria. Most importantly, if they wanted to sell their city-developed home within ten years, they had to first offer it back to the City at their original price, plus their equity, so that the City could make the property available to another eligible family.

West Loch Estates is a model affordable community built with greenbelts, parks and recreational amenities.

Model homes, tree-lined streets and an aerial view of the Model Village at West Loch, Phase I.

44

West Loch Estates transformed a neglected and polluted shoreline into beautiful biking and jogging paths.

West Loch Elderly Housing, one of the City's many affordable housing projects.

With the 1990s came Hawaii's recession and both the price and demand for housing withered. Homes being developed by the private sector were now priced at affordable levels, putting the City in the inappropriate role of being in direct competition with private housing developers.

Given the new market realities, the City phased out its housing department and returned the job of housing development to the private sector.

While the West Loch Estates project was a model for its time, it failed from an important sustainability perspective. The food stores and commercial shops that were designed to be part of the project were never built. As a result, this model community was still automobile-dependent.

Today, the price and demand for housing is again skyrocketing and government's role, if any, in dealing with the situation is being discussed.

Some have suggested that we reduce the price of new homes by eliminating the fees that government charges developers for such infrastructure as sewers and water.

City elderly housing for senior citizens in Manoa.

These ideas, while well intentioned, would have no impact on new housing prices and would only result in shifting these costs unfairly to other taxpayers. The median price of a new home on Oahu at this writing is $450,000. That price is not determined by the cost to build the home but by what the market will bear. Reducing fees won't reduce housing prices, it will just increase profits.

If government decides to get back into the housing business, it must do so cautiously. First of all, we shouldn't develop more single-family subdivisions. They only perpetuate the automobile culture and use up our finite amount of open land. If government is going to develop housing, it should be multi-family condominiums and rentals in the primary urban center and in Kapolei. With current construction prices, condominiums can be built that are affordable to Gap Group families without the need for subsidy.

Our collective vision for a sustainable island must include the best practices in land use. Concentrating development where we have existing roads, schools, and utilities makes good economic sense. Preserving open space for future generations and promoting self-sufficiency through agriculture are essential from a sustainability standpoint, and are vital to the livability of our community.

The first streetcar of Hawaiian Tramways Company, 1888 (Bishop Museum). Horse-drawn trolleys were eventually replaced by electric-powered trolleys, cuting travel time from Downtown Honolulu to Waikiki by one-third, Circa 1930 - 1940 (Hawaii State Archives). The electric streetcar debuted on August 31, 1901 (J.R. Baker, Hawaii State Archives).

Chapter 4
Sustainable Transportation

Land use policy dictates transportation policy. In Honolulu when we made the fatal mistake of building bedroom communities and separating people from their workplace, we locked ourselves into the need for freeways and automobiles. If we're to build a truly sustainable city, this fundamental mistake needs to be corrected.

Honolulu's history as it relates to transportation is sad. At one time, Honolulu had an excellent transportation system. We had trolleys with all the supporting infrastructure and dedicated rights of way connecting many parts of our island. We also had a narrow-gauge railroad, the OR&L, which circled most of the island. Unfortunately, shortsighted City leaders let this valuable transportation infrastructure be destroyed and replaced by the car culture.

Since then, we've learned that cities with light-rail systems, such as those Honolulu once had, are better able to meet the challenges of urban mobility than cities that rely solely on the automobile. To replace the light-rail systems that once graced this island will now cost hundreds of millions of dollars.

The City and County of Honolulu's involvement in mass transportation began over 30 years ago when then Mayor Frank Fasi flew to Texas and returned with used buses to begin the City's first bus system, replacing the privately owned HRT. The City found that Honolulu was well suited for mass transit, and the bus had a high ridership. But even in the early 70s the city realized that the needs of the growing population couldn't be met by buses alone. It was clear that a rail-transit system was needed.

As a result, Honolulu Area Rapid Transit (HART) was born. After years of study and work, a heavy-rail system was designed for the island and received federal approval and partial funding. However, in a move that would come to typify Honolulu's inability to reach consensus on a transportation solution, the HART project was cancelled by a new mayor in 1980. As a result, Honolulu lost the federal funds.

Four years later, when Mayor Fasi returned to the Mayor's Office, rail was back on the table. Years of work ensued, to design and plan a light-rail system for Honolulu that would carry people along the congested southern corridor. Because of its innovative procurement plan, Honolulu's design-build project became the model for the nation and rose to the top of the federal-funding list.

Once again, after years of study, research, planning and design, over $600 million in federal funds was set aside for the Honolulu project. But once again, Honolulu lost its political will, voted down local funding for the project, and in so doing lost the federal funds.

Despite having received the support of the congressional delegation, the Governor and both houses of the State Legislature, the City Council changed its mind about the funding for the rail system several weeks before construction was slated to begin. After more than two decades of study, analysis, and engineering, the City and County of Honolulu was left with no rail system and no consensus on a transportation plan.

In the meantime, TheBus had continued to grow, both in vehicle count, as well as in the number of communities served. But while TheBus was carrying over 70 million riders a year, it was reaching its limit to meet the needs of Honolulu's growing population.

An integrated transportation plan for the entire island needed to be developed, and that plan needed to be based on community input and support. This new community planning initiative was dubbed, "Trans 2-K"--Transportation For The Year 2000 and Beyond--and it involved an exhaustive series of island-wide meetings, gathering ideas and input from all sectors of the community.

Community Planning. Mayor Jeremy Harris and community members discuss energy, transportation and land use issues as key elements of a sustainable city.

The integrated transportation plan that resulted from the Trans 2-K community effort was based on a number of important principles.

First, the goal was to provide good mobility for the Honolulu urban core. The land use plan, designed to stop urban sprawl, required the redirection of much of the island's population growth to the primary urban center. To make our downtown area a great place to work and attractive to potential residents, it was important that the area provide good mobility and easy access.

Second, the transportation plan that was developed needed to recognize many of the key planning decisions that have been made for the future of our island. Keeping the country, country and reclaiming the waterfront were high priorities and needed to be supported by the transportation plan.

The third principle of the plan was called the "no silver bullet" rule. It recognized that to truly meet the transportation needs of our island community we needed to take a systems approach to the problem. Many things needed to be done. There was no single "silver bullet" that was going to solve the problem.

Finally, and perhaps most importantly, the plan had to be designed to make it easier to get from population centers around the island to downtown workplaces. It was especially important to move people from Central Oahu to Downtown and Waikiki and to connect the new second city in Kapolei to urban Honolulu.

The greening of Punchbowl Street, Ala Moana Boulevard and other City streets is part of the comprehensive plan to expedite the movement of traffic through the City by improving freeway access.

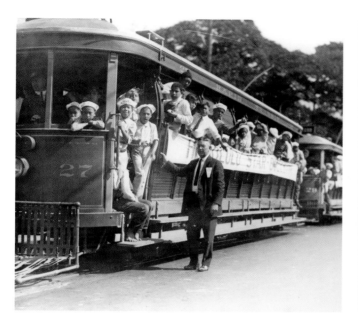

TheBus was named North America's best transit system and every bus was outfitted to carry bicycles. Top Left: Streetcar outing for "The Honolulu Star Bulletin" newsboys, Circa 1920, (Hawaii State Archives). Top Right: Bus washing, Circa 1971 (Bob Young, Honolulu Star-Bulletin, State Archives).

After more than a year of community input and expert analysis, the Trans 2K planning process yielded a comprehensive plan to improve mobility on the island. The City won a national award for this community planning initiative. The comprehensive plan called for intersection-by-intersection improvements to expedite the movement of traffic through the city. The transformation of Punchbowl Street can be attributed to this program. The plan also called for the expanded use of technology for traffic management, and the conversion of The Bus to a hub and spoke system.

But the centerpiece of the plan was the development of a Bus Rapid Transit (BRT) system for the island. BRT was chosen because it could carry as many passengers as a light rail system but could be built for a fraction of the cost. The system would be built incrementally as the City could afford it, with no increase in taxes needed to fund its construction.

Unlike the earlier rail transit plans that required large infrastructure development, and in many cases, elevated viaducts, the new bus rapid transit plan anticipated using surplus capacity on H-1 to accommodate the high-occupancy transit vehicles. A critical component of the plan was the development of both morning and afternoon zipper lanes with direct access for high-occupancy transit vehicles. The plan also included strategically located transit centers in communities along Oahu's southern shore.

With the reconfiguration of the bus into a hub and spoke system, people would be able to move conveniently from their home to a transit center, and from a transit center on to a Bus-Rapid Transit hybrid electric bus for the trip to Downtown and Waikiki.

The BRT plan also had an important component to provide the mobility so critical to the revitalization of Downtown. The first BRT segment was designed to run from Downtown past Aloha Tower, through the growth areas of Kakaako and into the main employment center of Waikiki.

Although the regional portion of the BRT system ran into roadblocks, the construction of the Downtown to Waikiki phase was achieved in 2004. Finally, after more than 35 years of bickering and indecision, a major transit project on Oahu had been constructed.

As the debates over transit continue, improvements to the bus are constantly made. The conversion of the bus to a hub and spoke system, and the addition of new transit centers greatly improved service. Country express routes with articulated buses were initiated, dramatically shortening the travel time to Downtown Honolulu for residents of West Oahu. New cutting-edge technology was employed to improve the comfort and efficiency of the bus system. All of the city's buses were converted to smart buses, where each bus was equipped with a global positioning system in contact with satellites in space. With this new technology, the bus itself knows exactly where it is on the streets of Honolulu, and without intervention from the driver, can announce to riders the upcoming stops.

Because of this and other technological and service improvements, Honolulu's bus system has twice been ranked the best transit system in North America.

Honolulu has always been committed to its handicapped riders as well. Not only are all of the city's buses equipped with wheelchair lifts and other accessibility features, but the City provides one of the country's most heavily utilized handi-van systems, providing door-to-door transportation service for citizens with physical disabilities.

Technology has played an important role in improving transportation throughout the island. In the 1990s, the city developed a computerized traffic control center that synchronized traffic lights to optimize the flow of automobiles through the city. It initiated an elaborate array of traffic cameras on all key arterials, so that every commuter could tune in on television or log on to the City Web site and see the state of traffic congestion on the various roads around the island before setting off on their commute.

The City's latest technological innovation is the hybrid electric bus, which will ultimately replace the diesel fleet. The first segment of the bus rapid transit system will be powered by this new technology. These buses will reduce emissions by 90 percent; improve fuel economy by 50 percent, and be virtually silent on our streets.

TheTransit. The City's new hybrid electric Bus Rapid Transit system represents a sustainable transportation technology for Honolulu.

Traffic Control Center. Synchronized traffic signals and video monitors on key arterials are part of the City's high-tech approach to traffic management.

Sometimes urban solutions involve low technology, not just high technology, and that's where the bicycle comes in. The City has developed a master plan to make Honolulu the most bicycle friendly city in the nation. City buses have been equipped with bicycle racks so that people can ride their bike to work and take the bus home, or simply bring their bike to work with them so they can peddle around the city during the day.

To further support a culture of bicycling, the City is aggressively building bike lanes connecting various parts of urban Honolulu, and is developing bike racks in every neighborhood.

Chapter 5

Energy

Civilization's Biggest Blunders

If you were to list civilization's largest blunders, our commitment to oil and coal for power generation and transportation fuel would have to rank near the top. Instead of developing renewable energy resources when it became obvious that fossil fuels were devastating our global environment, we allowed the oil industry to continue to dictate energy policy. This single mistake has had a profound impact on the cities of the world.

Not only did the automobile drive the habitation patterns and structure of our cities, but our reliance on fossil fuels has left many cities almost unlivable, with a legacy of air pollution, acid rain and respiratory disease.

Now our environment is threatened with global warming caused by the release of greenhouse gases from our gluttonous consumption of fossil fuels. Only a handful of the most shameless oil industry shills continue to question the relationship between the skyrocketing increase in the combustion of oil and coal and the dramatic atmospheric rise in the levels of carbon dioxide, a by-product of that combustion.

Despite their protestations, the facts are the facts – the world is getting warmer and cities are at the center of the problem. Urban land use, transportation and energy policies have caused this crisis, and dramatic urban policy shifts are the only hope of solving it.

The main cause of the problem is fossil fuel-based urban transportation systems. Cities need to re-tool and provide their citizens with affordable, convenient transportation alternatives that are less polluting. Efficient mass transit powered by hybrid electric or fuel cell technology needs to replace gasoline-powered cars.

Every city needs to go through this transformation – including Honolulu.

Honolulu's Energy History

As Honolulu was entering the 20th century, energy was easily available to provide light, fuel, transportation, and to cool the homes of island residents.

Around 1879, gaslights were gradually replaced by electric ones, and public transportation switched to electric trolleys, relegating "horse" power into the history books. In the 1930s, trolleys were shuttled aside in favor of electric buses with rubber tires.

These buses were not on rails and had more freedom to move around the streets, but they still were tied to their overhead power supply. Some of Honolulu's transportation system, however, was on rails. The OR&L (Oahu Rail and Land), a steam engine narrow gauge railroad, carried passengers from Honolulu to Kahuku by way of Kaena Point. The trip was scenic and grand, but it all came to an end in 1942.

In the 1950s, Honolulu switched from electric to diesel powered, free roaming city buses. New routes were opened up and diesel powered mass transit with limitless amounts of cheap fuel available, was here to stay – or so it seemed.

The late 1960s and 70s saw the explosion of highway construction on the island and the proliferation of automobiles. More visionary segments of our community pleaded for the money to be spent on rapid transit, but the road lobby was stronger.

Oahu's transit history. Above: King Street scene as viewed from Fort Street, Circa 1923-1924 (State Archives). Nuuanu Valley tram, Circa 1910. (Alonzo Gallery, Bishop Museum). Trolley, Circa 1923 (Hawaii State Archives). Below: Phase One – Hybrid Electric Bus Rapid Transit.

An unimaginative state government blundered ahead, chopping neighborhoods in half and paving over sacred valleys with more and more highway construction. The commitment to the car culture was complete. State government's chance to lay the foundation for a sustainable transportation energy policy was lost in a sea of myopia and mediocrity.

The commitment to automobile transportation contributed as well to an ever-increasing demand for energy. Today, transportation consumes 70 percent of our energy pie. In the 1990s, and again at the turn of the 21st century, fear, instability and war in the Middle East sent oil prices spiraling upward, just as demand was peaking.

Honolulu's roads became so clogged that daily commuting time began to be measured in hours instead of minutes. Energy consumption in the form of imported fossil fuels surged ahead like a tsunami.

At the same time, trade winds and fans were no longer cool enough for Honolulu's office workers and retail stores. Air conditioning, with its heavy demand for electricity became the norm. The growth of imported fossil fueled electrical power grew apace.

The City and County's dependence on imported oil to fuel lighting, commuting, and cooling had reached an unsustainable level. During this time, to make things even worse, the City's income, based on property taxes, was declining.

The Japanese property buying frenzy of the late 80s, which drove up property values and city income, had come to an end. Property values plummeted sending tax revenue to the sub-basement. The City saw its tax income drop by $178 million from 1994 to 2000.

With income at its lowest in a decade and energy costs skyrocketing, the City established a plan called "Sustainable Honolulu." The idea was to lead by example. City Hall would create new programs and procedures to ensure a high quality of life for residents based on environmental protection and energy self-sufficiency.

The Energy Plan, which calls for cutting Honolulu's energy demand at city facilities in half by 2010, consisted of three main approaches. The first was to retrofit all city facilities so they would be more energy efficient. The second approach was to establish distributed energy systems so buildings would generate their own power and reduce their need for electricity from the grid. The final and most important part of the plan was to reduce reliance on fossil fuels and develop renewable energy sources to meet city needs.

To serve as a model, what better place to start than Honolulu Hale itself? Hundreds of incandescent lights were replaced with compact and energy efficient fluorescents, saving on electric costs. A new co-generation power plant was installed. Powered by syngas and using waste heat to cool the building, the co-generation plant is 93 percent efficient and reduces Honolulu Hale's electricity demand by a whopping 70 percent.

Energy Efficiency. Honolulu Hale's grid electricity demand has been cut by seventy percent by implementing energy efficient lighting and developing a co-generation power plant for the building.

These energy efficient solutions reduce demand for electricity at City Hall, but the really good news is that the projects pay for themselves with the energy savings they create. Similar retrofits for the Honolulu Municipal Building and the main police station on Beretania Street are underway.

No stone was left unturned in the search for energy efficiency. All the island's traffic signals were converted from incandescent bulbs to light emitting diodes (LED), lowering the City's electric bill by a quarter million dollars each year. And at Hanauma Bay, LED parking lot lights powered by miniature wind turbines and photovoltaic cells have been installed. Since the new energy efficient lights last 40 times longer than normal bulbs, their maintenance cost is far less and millions more dollars are saved.

Over the next year, private firms will install a minimum of two megawatts of solar electric power at City facilities around the island. This "electricity from the sun" will dramatically reduce our need to purchase electricity from Hawaiian Electric and the technology will be paid for by the private sector energy company that installs it. We save money on our electric bill, they share our savings, and together we help the planet.

The City has also embarked on a new "Bio-Power Initiative" to retrofit our wastewater treatment plants with biogas energy systems. Treatment plant methane will be used to generate electricity for the plants, further reducing the City's electric bill by millions of dollars each year.

Additionally, the City has installed methane collection systems at two of our landfills, which together have generated enough power for more than 200 homes.

Perhaps the most innovative effort in renewable energy is the City's planned development of a Hydrogen Power Park at Kapolei Hale. This cutting-edge program will feature an array of photovoltaic cells as a canopy over the parking lot. The electricity generated will be used to produce hydrogen through the electrolysis of water. By converting solar energy to hydrogen, the energy can be stored and used when it's needed to run a hydrogen co-generation system that will power the building. Fueling stations for hydrogen vehicles and electric vehicles and a fuel cell test bed will complete the facility.

The Hydrogen Power Park is a unique partnership with the State Energy Office, the U.S. Department of Energy, the Hawaii Natural Energy Institute, and numerous private firms. This initiative will save taxpayers money in the form of lower electric bills, and make Honolulu a world leader in hydrogen technology.

The ocean itself can be a source of renewable energy. The Board of Water Supply has teamed up with the University of Hawaii Medical School to develop an innovative district cooling system for the new Kakaako bio-medical campus. The project will reduce water usage and electrical consumption to air condition the medical facilities. A deep well has been drilled along the Kakaako coast, tapping into cold ocean water.

Cold seawater will be used to provide the cooling for the medical school's air conditioning needs and in so doing, will eliminate the waste of 23 million gallons of fresh water each year that would otherwise be needed in traditional air-conditioning technology.

In addition to shifting to electricity generated by renewable energy, the City has also turned its sustainable energy focus to transportation.

With a fleet of over a thousand vehicles, the City uses lots of fuel. In the past, most of the City's fleet was powered by diesel fossil fuel. Now, over a thousand of the City's refuse trucks and maintenance vehicles are run on bio-diesel, manufactured from recycled vegetable oil. To encourage the private use of biodiesel, the City has cut the County fuel tax in half for this fuel.

Instead of clogging our sewers, waste french fry oil is blended with diesel to power our vehicles and reduce our consumption of fossil diesel by 20 percent. Bio-diesel burns cleaner, lubricates better, produces less soot and smoke, and reduces cancer-causing emissions. On top of all that, it smells like french fries when the trucks go by.

By running trucks on used vegetable oil and deploying hybrid electric buses in the new bus rapid transit system, the City is hoping to serve as a model for how Hawaii's flawed energy policy can be corrected.

Bio Diesel. Over 1,000 of the City's trucks are now powered by bio-diesel made from waste cooking oil.

Renewable Energy Resources. Honolulu is blessed with abundant renewable energy resources that can be developed to reduce dependence on imported fossil fuels.

But leading by example isn't enough. To put some teeth in the City's new energy policy, we have adopted a model energy code that codifies energy efficiency regulations for all new construction and major renovations. The reduction in energy usage that will result from these new lighting, insulation, and building design laws will save taxpayers more than $300 million in coming years.

Just because our State and City made the wrong energy policy decisions in the past, doesn't mean we need to continue these mistakes. Honolulu is blessed with abundant renewable energy resources and an island transportation system that we can control. The only thing standing in the way of becoming a model for the world in energy sustainability is ourselves.

Recreating a Hawaiian sense of place. A lane of traffic on Kalakaua Avenue was replaced with lush landscaping, water features and wide walkways to enhance the strolling experience along Waikiki Beach, sparking the revitalization of the tourist economy.

Chapter 6
The Economy

Hawaii – Pawn or Planner?

The economic pillars of Hawaii's economy have never been pre-planned.   Economic development has always been something that has "happened to" Hawaii rather than having been "chosen by" Hawaii. This is true of the rise of plantation agriculture, the growth of the military economy after WWII, and the tourism boom following the development of transpacific air travel.

It wasn't until the Jack Burns era that a plan for Hawaii's economic future was articulated and a vision for Hawaii's role in the Asia-Pacific region was defined. Governor Burns foresaw Hawaii's future as the gateway between East and West.

He recognized our strategic advantage as a multi-cultural, multi-lingual, Central-Pacific community. He correctly identified our potential as a center for science and technology.

Unfortunately, while the pre-Burns Hawaii was characterized by no economic future planning, post-Burns Hawaii has been characterized by just the opposite—all planning and little effective action.

Sugar as King

The economy of Honolulu today is very different from the economy of 100 years ago. As we entered the 20th Century, sugar was king and the barons of the sugar industry had total control over the economic, social, and political reins of Honolulu. Plantation agriculture was the only game in town, and its influence touched every aspect of local society.

Seminal decisions were made by this elite group of entrepreneurs. Their importation of plantation workers from foreign lands would forever establish the multi-cultural diversity of Hawaii. Their placement and development of plantation camps would later evolve into our island towns, and their governance of these islands would determine Hawaii's future geopolitical position in the world. The plantation economy forever transformed this island—its people, its land use, its environment, and its politics. Although the plantations are now gone, victims to the most expensive agricultural land and labor in the world, their impact on Honolulu is indelible.

The sugar industry transformed Honolulu's economic, social and political destiny. Plantation workers from foreign lands established the cultural diversity in Hawaii (Hawaii State Archives). The Oahu Railway & Land (OR&L) train hauled sugar cane from Ewa to the processing plant, Circa 1890s (Hawaii State Archives).

Military Money

The importance of the military to Honolulu's economy grew appreciably during and after the Second World War.   Thousands of Hawaii's men and women found stable, well paid careers in the federal government. A job at "the shipyard" was synonymous with good benefits and lifelong tenure.

During the Vietnam War, Honolulu's military economy continued to grow. Designated as an R&R destination, streets were alive with soldiers, sailors, airmen and marines fresh from the war zone. In a matter of hours, America's young military men and women could find themselves transported from the jungles of Indochina to the streets of Waikiki and Chinatown.

The military presence in Honolulu, although not universally praised, continued to provide stability to our economy. Many thought it was a sector that would continue to grow perpetually. Yet, because of a number of factors, the size of the workforce at Pearl Harbor was slowly reduced and Barbers Point Naval Air Station was closed in 1999.

With the end of the Cold War and the reconfiguration of the American military, new plans have emerged for a greatly expanded military presence on Oahu.

This expansion may or may not be good for our island community. In any case, it should be something we decide after thoughtful community dialogue. The benefits and impact, not just economic, but social, and cultural as well, need to be fully vetted. The result needs to be something we desire and plan for instead of something that simply "happens to us."

Unsustainable Tourism

The growth of tourism after the war transformed Oahu almost as dramatically as the plantations had. With direct airline flights, tourists flocked to the island, and Waikiki scrambled to keep up. Unfortunately, the City's planning process was slow to respond, and Waikiki, which could have been developed as one of the world's finest cultural resort destinations, was allowed to grow haphazardly. The result was a disaster and the word "Waikiki" in many people's minds became synonymous with "bad development."

Trees were cut down, cheap undistinguished walk-up apartments went up and sidewalks were littered with shoddy touristy gew-gaws.

For many years, tourism grew in an unsustainable way. People traveled from around the world to experience the Hawaiian culture and enjoy our pristine environment. Yet in developing tourism, development was destroying the very things visitors were coming to experience.

Waikiki – Before and After. Poor urban design characterized Waikiki until the late 1990s when it was transformed with water features, landscaping and meandering walkways.

Honolulu's pristine environment was being damaged. We were polluting our streams and ocean with sewage and urban runoff, and littering our landscape with garbage. We allowed subdivisions to march across open agricultural lands, and environmental jewels such as Hanauma Bay to be exploited and abused.

The Hawaiian culture faired no better than the environment in the tourism onslaught. The unique cultural experience people were coming to enjoy was cheapened and mass-produced. Visitors seeking authenticity found only parody.

By the 1990s, Honolulu had lost its "Hawaiian sense of place."

A Vulnerable Economy

With the demise of plantation agriculture and the reduction of military spending, Honolulu became overly dependant on tourism as its economic base. This placed the island in a vulnerable economic position. The fragility caused by this lack of economic diversity became painfully apparent when the Japanese bubble economy burst in the mid 1990s.

Many Japanese visitors stopped coming to Honolulu because of the bad economy and Waikiki hotels suffered with low occupancy. The collapsing Japanese economy also signaled the demise of Japanese speculation in Honolulu real estate. In a few short years, property values on Oahu plummeted by almost $20 billion.

The folly of being overly dependent on tourism was further magnified on September 11, 2001. After the terrorist attack, international tourists were hesitant to travel to U.S. destinations and many were fearful of air travel. The impact on Waikiki was immediate and severe. The terrorist attack of September 11th was the final alarm for tourism, but not the first.

By the end of the 80s, tourism was already hurting. Waikiki, the economic engine of the State, was looking tired and run down. It was an aging beach resort, and visitors were not returning. Public infrastructure was shabby and private sector retail and hotel stock had not been upgraded in many years. Waikiki was described as a "mature" destination that had to re-invent itself or risk dying of old age.

By the mid 1990's, Waikiki had lost more than its youth; it had lost its Hawaiian sense of place. Years of inattention to urban design, landscaping, and cultural heritage had turned Waikiki into "Anywhere USA."

The architecture was a haphazard polyglot of styles that had no relevance to Hawaii. The streetlights and traffic signals looked like they came from a Los Angeles freeway. And the entire peninsula was designed to accommodate automobile through traffic, not pedestrians.

Visitors coming from around the world to sample the Hawaiian arts and culture discovered there was none to be found in Waikiki. You could see "Elvis" or "Marilyn Monroe," but never a local *hula halau* performing native dance.

The experience offered to our guests was not authentic. Today's travelers are far too sophisticated to settle for a canned *luau* and a Tahitian dance. Surveys of Japanese tourists found that they strongly objected to signage in Waikiki that was in Japanese. They wanted the signs to be in Hawaiian. And all visitors were uniformly disappointed that during their stay in Waikiki, they never got to meet any people from Hawaii.

Conversely, when local residents were polled, they frequently expressed the opinion that they weren't welcome in Waikiki, that it was only for the tourists.

Something needed to be done.

The Plan for Economic Recovery

To deal with the island's faltering economy, the City developed a straightforward plan that was short on rhetoric and long on action.

The first step of the plan was to bolster our core economy by revitalizing Waikiki. The second step was to diversify our tourism base so that visitors would come to our island for more than the Waikiki experience. The visitor markets the City targeted were sports tourism, eco-tourism, and cultural/edu-tourism.

The final component of the plan was to build the economy in the area of knowledge-based industries, taking advantage of Honolulu's unique expertise in environmental science and technology.

Revitalizing Waikiki

The revitalization of Waikiki was a massive undertaking involving both the public and private sectors. To inspire private investors to upgrade their hotels and shops, the City first had to spark a rebirth of Waikiki by revitalizing public areas.

Any change in Hawaii meets stiff opposition, but proposing to replace traffic lanes with trees and water features is almost suicidal. Nevertheless, change was needed, so the battles were waged, and the lawsuits fought.

In the end, most of the City's plans survived and the rebirth of Waikiki could begin.

The first step of the revitalization needed to be symbolic so the community could get a positive sense of improvements to come. What better icon to first attack than the ugly brown "L.A. Freeway" lights and traffic signals?

Historic Lighting and Flowers. The first step in Waikiki's revitalization was the replacement of the modernistic streetlights with historic lighting fixtures with hanging flower pots.

Designing for people first – not cars. One lane of Kalakaua Avenue was bulldozed and replaced by trees, flowers and pedestrian walkways.

Bringing the park into the City. Kapiolani Park was brought into Waikiki providing tree shaded grassy lawns for beach goers and a park-like experience along Kuhio Beach.

Out they came, replaced by historic lighting and hanging flower baskets. The reaction was immediate and positive and Waikiki's transformation gathered support.

The next challenge was the revitalization of Kuhio Beach. One of our over-reaching goals was to make Waikiki more of a pedestrian place, with fewer cars and more opportunities for locals and visitors to stroll along the waterfront.

Although it was one of the most famous beaches in the world, Kuhio had become a pretty dismal place. The four-lane Kalakaua Avenue came right up to the beach, separated in many places by only a narrow sidewalk and yellow guardrails. Porta-potties blighted the street, and in the evenings, the area was abandoned to panhandlers and the homeless.

The plan called for taking out the makai lane of Kalakaua and bringing Kapiolani Park into Waikiki. For the first time, Waikiki Beach was fronted with grass, trees and flowers.

The revitalization of Kuhio Beach was grounded in a commitment to pedestrians over cars. Asphalt roadway was replaced by quartzite paved meandering walkways, native Hawaiian landscaping, and flowerbeds.

People places were created and the Kapahulu groin was transformed into the Kapahulu Pier, with a lovely pavilion at its terminus.

Putting Pedestrians First. Flowers brighten the streetscape along Waikiki Beach.

Kuhio Beach – Before and After. Concrete pavement and iron railings were replaced with grass lawns, coconut palms, park benches and more sandy beach.

Providing shade and a gathering place, the charming pavilion became a magnet for local children enjoying the waves and for visitors seeking a romantic vantage point to enjoy the ocean and the Waikiki shoreline.

Waterfalls and tidal pools were created all along the Kalakaua promenade providing lovely places for visitors to have their pictures taken and for children to wash off their sandy feet.

The old food concession and police station were demolished and replaced with new facilities that more appropriately reflected the architecture of Hawaii.

It's not just Prince Kuhio's beachfront namesake that has been revitalized. Kuhio Avenue, the heart of residential Waikiki, has been transformed as well.

The strip of land from Kuhio Avenue to the Ala Wai has always been Waikiki's residential community. Princess Kaiulani and Robert Lewis Stevenson both called the area home.

Over the years, however, as the tourist industry grew, Kuhio Avenue became more and more the back service ally of commercial Waikiki. This unfortunate transformation was complete with the widening of Kuhio in the early 1980s.

Pedestrian and residential needs were ignored as sidewalks were narrowed to provide more space for delivery trucks and tour buses.

The old "jungle," a residential neighborhood of little lanes and small buildings, was largely wiped out as a new five-lane concrete Kuhio Avenue was punched through to Kapahulu.

The rebirth of Kuhio signaled the avenue's return to focusing on the pedestrian. Coupled with the new hybrid electric Bus Rapid Transit system improvements, the transformation of Kuhio included wider meandering sidewalks paved with stone, the planting of grass and trees, and historic lighting with hanging flower baskets.

Waikiki was designed to be the Venice of the Pacific. The Ala Wai Canal was built in the 1920s to drain the low-lying wetlands. The dredge spoils were piled on the Waikiki lands to increase their elevation and value.

The original plans called for making Waikiki an island, and the old easements that show the Ala Wai cutting through Kapiolani Park and entering the ocean near the Waikiki Aquarium are still on the maps.

Unfortunately, the recreational and aesthetic potential of the Ala Wai was never fully realized. The canal was always popular with outrigger canoe paddlers, and in the early days, a small boat rental operated at the McCully Bridge for romantic couples willing to brave the polluted water. Through the 1970s, fishing chairs on stilts dotted the waters edge and some of us who were less prudent actually dove off the bridge into the canal to cool off on hot days. Other than these few uses, the Ala Wai never achieved its "Venice" billing.

Waikiki Water Features. One of the most photographed sites on Oahu is now the beautifully landscaped waterfall on Kuhio Beach.

As part of the Bus Rapid Transit project, Kuhio Avenue was made more pedestrian friendly with meandering walkways and landscaping.

Honolulu has received the designation as Tree City, U.S.A.

Ala Wai Canal and Boulevard landscaping and bikeway improvements.

As the sump for all the runoff from the mauka valleys, the Ala Wai silted in quickly and became the storehouse of the most polluted water and sediment on the island. Finally, after years of study and permitting, the State dredged the canal in 2003. In recent years, activities have been encouraged on the Ala Wai. The Toro Nagashi floating lantern ceremony and rowing regatta now draw visitors and locals to its banks.

To further promote the canal's recreational use, the city has widened areas of the landscaped strip along the boulevard, and planted grass, flowers, and coconut palms. Historic lighting has been added and a bikeway has been constructed along its entire length so more people can enjoy the canal.

The Ala Wai Canal's potential has only begun to be realized. Water taxis, outdoor dining, and boat rentals could help transform this once open drainage channel into the aesthetic and recreational heart of Waikiki.

The Cultural Renaissance

For tourism to be sustainable, it must nourish the local culture. Not doing harm is not enough. Tourism needs to promote and celebrate the host culture and provide support and resources for its perpetuation.

Part of the effort to expand our cultural tourism economy has been the establishment of Honolulu as the Festival City of the Pacific. Ethnic celebrations have long been part of the fabric of Honolulu life. The Okinawa Festival, Filipino Fiesta, and Aloha Week festivities are just a few of the wonderful cultural programs that our visitors share when they visit our shores.

The City has worked with community groups in recent years to expand these cultural activities. New events have been created, such as the Dragon Boat Festival staged around the colorful dragon boat races at Ala Moana Beach Park and the Paniola Festival that celebrates Hawaii's cowboy heritage with roping and riding events.

To provide opportunities for more cultural events in Waikiki, a hula performance mound was created under the historic banyan tree. Now visitors can enjoy local dance and music performances every night at Kuhio Beach. The nightly torch-lighting ceremony at Kuhio and the accompanying hula performance attract hundreds of thousands of people each year.

Visitors crave authenticity. As they walk the streets of our exotic city, they want to learn more about the history and people of Hawaii. In the past, our guests were greeted by a confusing array of street and place names, all four or five syllables long and all seeming to start with the letter 'K.'

The Paniola (Hawaiian Cowboy) Festival is one of many that make Honolulu a great city of festivals.

The city of Kaohsiung, Taiwan gave dragon boats to the City and County of Honolulu to commemorate its Sister City relationship and establish annual Dragon Boat Races at Ala Moana Beach Park.

In 2004, the 10th Annual Honolulu Festival and the 25th Pan-Pacific Festival brought thousands of artists and participants from Japan to Honolulu, generating millions for our economy and offering special cultural events for residents and visitors.

The City's Torch Lighting Ceremony and Hula Show at Kuhio Beach is the only traditional Hawaiian hula performance visitors may experience nightly.

106

So that visitors could appreciate the important personages of Honolulu's past who had helped mold this island, artists were commissioned to create bronze sculptures of the people behind the place names. Kaiulani, Kuhio, Kalakaua, Kapiolani and Kahanamoku came alive and the locations named for them took on new meaning.

Waikiki's cultural renaissance didn't end with the development of the hula performance mound.

The main performance center in Waikiki had long been the Kapiolani Park Bandstand. Home of the Royal Hawaiian Band and a variety of cultural events, the old bandstand could be described, at best, as dilapidated. Designed like a WWII gun emplacement, the old bandstand fell dismally short of projecting the cultural charm of Hawaii. Audiences were forced to sit in the sun on muddy ground, or provide their own beach chairs. In short, the Kapiolani Park Bandstand was a disgrace. This was not always the case. Near the turn of the 20th Century, a lovely Victorian bandstand set amidst lily ponds and lush greenery graced the park. To recapture that lost charm, the City set out to replace the old bandstand with a new performance center in keeping with the park's romantic past.

A beautiful new bandstand was designed, suggestive of its Victorian heritage and nestled around a lovely pond. Opposition and threatened lawsuits quickly erupted at the suggestion of more change for Waikiki. Opponents were convinced the ponds would be mosquito breeding grounds and that the hapless public would stumble in and drown. But in the end, common sense prevailed and the project was built.

Kapiolani Park Bandstand.   Top right: The Royal Hawaiian Band at Makee island bandstand, Circa 1900 (R.W. Leonard Collection, Hawaii State Archives).   The focal point of Queen Kapiolani Park, the bandstand has been transformed back to its original Victorian architectural style nestled in a lily pond.

108

Kapiolani Park Bandstand, dedicated in July 2001.

Dedicated on the Fourth of July, the Kapiolani Park Bandstand is the gathering place for colorful ethnic and cultural festivities.

With this new performance venue in Waikiki, the number and size of cultural events skyrocketed. People could now sit in comfortable seats under the protective branches of monkey pod trees to enjoy the best of Hawaii's multi-cultural performances.

The Natatorium

In order to be a truly sustainable tourism economy, we need to preserve and celebrate our history as well as our culture. Although it was hotly contested, the Kapiolani Park Bandstand wasn't the most controversial project in this historic revitalization of Waikiki. That title belongs to the Natatorium.

Opened in 1927 as a memorial to Hawaii's sons who fought and died in World War I, the Natatorium was the first living memorial in the United States. Not only do the heroic archways and eagles memorialize our veterans, but so too does the pool itself, with children and families swimming and playing.

Caught in a political squabble between the City and State in the 1970s, the Natatorium was allowed to deteriorate to such a point that it was closed in 1979.

A political hot potato, the pool sat for almost two decades behind a barrier of chain link and barbed wire. Everyone had a different idea about what should be done with the Natatorium, and so political leaders did nothing. Some said tear it down, not realizing that the pool walls captured the sand creating Kaimana Beach, and that if the Natatorium was demolished, the beach would be gone within months. Others said turn it into a volleyball court. Still others envisioned a performance center or an aquarium. The central fact that few seemed willing to acknowledge, however, was that the pool was a protected structure on both the State and National Historic registers. Only two options were available: let the historic memorial continue to deteriorate and fall eventually into the sea, or repair it.

The decision was simple, if controversial: repair it.

More opposition and lawsuits ensued and the courts intervened, only allowing the City to restore the bleachers and beach center building. As a result, public restrooms, lockers, and showers returned to the Natatorium along with the restored arches, but the pool restoration was stopped.

In a decision that left engineers and scientists scratching their heads, the court's ruling required, in essence, that the Natatorium be chlorinated. Since the salt-water pool was open on both sides to the Pacific Ocean, the size of the chlorination job looked formidable. Chemically, you can't chlorinate saltwater, and since the Pacific Ocean is a bit too large to chlorinate even if you could, the restoration of the historic war memorial was halted yet again.

The Natatorium. The first phase of restoration of this national historic site was re-dedicated on Memorial Day, 2000, to those who fought in World War I.

The fate of the memorial was again brought to the fore in the summer of 2004. This time the issue was not historic preservation or society's obligation to its war dead, but straightforward public safety. Large sections of the pool deck began to collapse into the sea, jeopardizing the lives of children who continue to climb the walls to play there. At this writing, the City has ordered emergency health and safety repairs, but more lawsuits have been filed. The fate of the Natatorium remains unresolved.

Waikiki – A Hawaiian Place

Home of the *alii* and burial place for Hawaiians since the days before contact, Waikiki is, above all, a Hawaiian place. Over the decades, as Waikiki developed, construction projects often unearthed the bones of ancient Hawaiians long ago buried in the soft sands of the coast. Instead of being treated with reverence, these *iwi kupuna* were often stored away in boxes.

As part of the rebirth of Waikiki, the families of the ancient Hawaiians whose *iwi* had been disturbed came together to plan a memorial site where their ancestor's bones could be respectfully re-interred and honored appropriately. This memorial to the *iwi kupuna* now graces the corner of Kapahulu and Kalakaua and stands as a moving reminder that we must never forget Hawaii's ancestral origins.

Nineteen bronze surfboards mark the rich history of Waikiki; another Waikiki Revitalization initiative to restore the Hawaiian sense of place to the destination.

To teach more visitors about the history of Waikiki and its people, bronze surfboard markers with historic information have been erected at selected sites throughout the peninsula. This historic trail allows locals and tourists to stroll through Waikiki and learn about its past.

Waikiki – A Great Place to Live

If a community is an exciting and enriching place to live, it's also a great place to visit. In order to break down the old barriers that left locals feeling that they weren't welcome in Waikiki, and had tourists complaining that they never got to meet the people of Hawaii, the City initiated two of the most popular events in Honolulu's history. "Sunset on the Beach" and "Brunch on the Beach" were designed to help turn Honolulu's economy around during one of the worst tourism slumps in our history. The idea was to provide authentic experiences where locals and tourists could come together, share a meal of local food, enjoy real Hawaiian entertainment and actually form relationships.

Brunch on the Beach was the first event to be tried. One Sunday each month, a portion of Kalakaua Avenue is closed down, covered with Astroturf, and liberally sprinkled with tables and festive umbrellas. The best restaurants in town bring their Victorian tents and best recipes, and thousands of people, locals and tourists alike, turn out to enjoy the best of food, fun, and Hawaiian entertainment.

Almost every weekend, Waikiki also plays host to Sunset on the Beach. Again, great food and entertainment are part of the festivities, but with Sunset comes a full-length motion picture shown right on the beach after the sun goes down.

If Sunset on the Beach isn't happening in Waikiki, it's probably on the road in another community on the island as part of the City's Rediscover Oahu economic development initiative. At long last, visitors and locals are coming together to share authentic island experiences. Since their inception, Brunch and Sunset have attracted over a million people and generated millions of dollars of economic activity for local businesses.

The City's investment in the rebuilding of Waikiki in recent years totals about $70 million, a relatively modest amount considering the area's importance as the island's economic engine. More significant, however, is the fact that the investment in public infrastructure has triggered over $1 billion of planned private sector re-development. The rebirth of Waikiki is ongoing, and this renaissance is characterized by the protection and enhancement of the environment and a respect for the Hawaiian culture. From architecture and urban design to culture and arts programs, the Hawaiian sense of place is returning to Waikiki.

Once a month on Sunday, Brunch on the Beach transforms Kalakaua Avenue into an outdoor café where thousands of residents and visitors enjoy signature dishes and great Hawaiian entertainment. Another Waikiki Revitalization initiative, Brunch also provides jobs for local entertainers and hula halau.

Celebrating the movie premiere of "Shark Tale", winners of a student art contest displayed their artwork and received their awards at a special Brunch on the Beach.

Since July 2001, thousands of residents and visitors have attended one of Honolulu's most popular special event, Brunch on the Beach. Executive Chef Fred DeAngelo and his son cook frittatas at the Tiki's Grill and Bar food station while the ladies of Halau Hula Olana share their aloha with guests at the popular event.

Thousands enjoy entertainment, local food and feature-length movies on a 30-foot screen as the sun sets at Queen's Surf Beach.

Crowds throng to Kapahulu Pier and Queen's Surf Beach for Sunset on the Beach.

The Rediscover Oahu program brings Sunset on the Beach to Waianae, Haleiwa, Waimanalo, Pearl City, Aiea and Kapolei.

Eco-Tourism

If we want to remain competitive in the tourist market, offering a great Waikiki experience isn't enough. We need to diversify our visitor industry into other niche markets, and eco-tourism provides us an opportunity to do so sustainably. By attracting visitors to our island to enjoy unique environmental experiences, we can grow our visitor industry as we protect and enhance our environmental assets. There is no better example of this principle than the story of Hanauma Bay.

Hanauma Bay

Long a popular fishing site, Hanauma Bay was designated a marine life conservation district in 1967. The designation stopped most of the fishing, but it did not protect the bay from its own burgeoning popularity.

This volcanic cinder cone turned coral reef became a "must see" for tourists who quickly overwhelmed it with tour buses and beach blankets. Too many people and too many cars destroyed the experience and threatened to destroy the bay itself.

The City's management of this environmental jewel can only be described as "third world". Ugly hollow tile buildings at the top of the crater and a termite eaten clapboard fast food restaurant down on the beach said it all.

Hanauma Bay. A collapsed volcanic cinder cone formed this magnificent crescent shaped bay thousands of years ago.

The award-winning Hanauma Bay Marine Education Center is part of the City's sustainable tourism strategy to protect Hawaii's natural heritage through eco-tourism.

126

Proclaimed the world's best beach, Hanauma Bay limits its number of visitors to protect its fragile coral reef.

Hanauma was treated as simply another beach. The City's vision was to transform Hanauma into a nature learning center and to limit the number of visitors going to the bay so that its reef wouldn't be damaged.

The old buildings at the top of the rim were torn down and replaced with an earth bermed Marine Education Center landscaped with native plants. Here, Hanauma's visitors and Honolulu's children could turn their trip to the bay into a learning experience about the geology, marine biology and volcanology of Hawaii.

Down at the beach, the old restrooms were removed and replaced by modern facilities hidden away within the rock face. The old fast food restaurant was razed and a simple thatched learning kiosk took its place. With careful management, Hanauma Bay can serve as both an ecotourism site and an educational learning center for Hawaii's children for generations to come.

Waimea Valley

If we are to continue to attract visitors to our island, we must preserve our cultural and environmental resources. Waimea Valley on the North Shore is one such resource.

Operated as a tourist stop for years, the valley environment was deteriorating. Off-road vehicles were eroding valley trails and important botanical specimens were suffering from a lack of maintenance. To protect the unique environmental, cultural and educational resource, the City purchased the valley and brought in the Audubon Society to operate it as a nature center.

Sports Tourism

In addition to eco-tourism, sports tourism held enormous potential to diversify our economy. Our superb climate and year round outdoor playing season, and our central location in the Asia-Pacific region, make Honolulu a natural venue for national and international sporting events. Already famous for such events as the Pro Bowl, the Sony Open, and the Honolulu Marathon, the only thing that was holding Honolulu back from further sports tourism success was a lack of athletic facilities.

The plan the City developed was designed to help the economy as well as local families. The concept was to develop world-class sporting venues that could attract national and international events to support the local economy. Since these major economic events would be intermittent, these excellent athletic facilities could be used by Oahu's families throughout most of the year.

The first project to be developed was the Waipio Penninsula Soccer Complex. Over 23,000 children on Oahu were involved in organized soccer, yet there were few fields available to accommodate their play. At the same time, lucrative soccer tournaments were going to other parts of the world, because Honolulu didn't have the facilities to host them.

The Waipio Soccer Complex, with 23 fields and a championship stadium, has welcomed more than a million visitors since its opening and is a centerpiece of the City's sports tourism program.

To meet this need and capitalize on this opportunity, a 35-field soccer complex with an accompanying soccer stadium was planned. Over 200 acres of land was made available by the military on Waipio Pennisula to accommodate the ambitious project, and the stadium and first 22 soccer fields were developed.

The facility was an instant success. National tournaments immediately booked into the new complex and the Waipio facility quickly became recognized as one of the best soccer facilities in the U.S. Waipio soccer tournaments pumped tens of millions of dollars into the Honolulu economy, and Oahu's children finally had high quality soccer fields to play on.

Central Oahu Regional Park

Soccer was only one of the sports that showed promise for sports tourism. Baseball, softball, tennis, and aquatics all presented opportunities for economic development and all represented activities in which the City lacked quality facilities. In addition to our immediate needs, it was obvious that the City also needed to set aside parkland for future population growth. After all, what would our urban quality of life be like today in Downtown Honolulu if leaders years ago hadn't had the vision to reserve land for Kapiolani Park and Ala Moana Beach Park?

The location chosen to meet these current and future park needs was the Central Oahu site known as Waiola.

The Central Oahu Regional Park Tennis Complex, named one of the top 5 tennis facilities in the United States, has been the site of numerous national, state and local championships.

Central Oahu Regional Park has hosted numerous state and local baseball and softball tournaments and served as an off-season training facility for professional teams from Asia.

Construction of the Tennis and Aquatics Center at Central Oahu Regional Park will provide Honolulu families with world-class recreational facilities while building a sustainable sports tourism industry.

134

Strategically located between Honolulu and Kapolei, this 269-acre site was over three times the size of Kapiolani Park. It would become the "central park" of Oahu.

Professional quality baseball fields were the first developed, followed by a softball quadraplex and acres of playing fields for soccer, lacrosse, and rugby. Next came the development of the 20 court tennis complex with show courts. On its opening day, Central Oahu hosted a prestigious USTA tournament and was proclaimed one of the top five tennis complexes in the U.S. Heavily utilized by local residents and tournaments alike, the tennis complex is maintained and operated by the non-profit Hawaii-Pacific Tennis Foundation. Soon to be completed at Central Oahu Regional Park is a world-class aquatic complex. The only one of its kind in the U.S., this facility allows Honolulu to attract national and international swimming and diving events to support the economy, while providing our local swim clubs with excellent facilities.

Also nearing completion is the clubhouse for the regional park. This facility provides shower and locker facilities and a lovely restaurant in a landscaped courtyard.

Knowledge-Based Industries

Strengthening and broadening our tourism industry with improvements in Waikiki and with new facilities for sports and eco-tourism has been only part of the City's strategy for economic development.

Building Honolulu's Ties with China. Mayor Jeremy Harris and The People's Republic of China President Jiang Zemin met in Honolulu in 1997. The City's goal is to develop knowledge-based industries that market Honolulu's expertise to Asian nations.

While tourism will always be important to our local economy, Honolulu's true destiny is to be an Asia-Pacific center for knowledge-based industries. The vision Governor Burns articulated 40 years ago, to make Hawaii a center for science and technology, is as valid today as it was then.

In the 21st century, the Asia-Pacific region is much different than it was in Burn's time. Today's Asia is urbanizing and industrializing at an alarming rate. The consumption of natural resources and the resulting pollution are suffocating Asia's cities and poisoning its rivers and ocean. Even Hawaii has begun to detect air pollution from China's coal-fired power plants.

The urban leaders of Asia are reeling under the challenges of urbanization and the ramifications of their actions or inaction are impacting us all.

This regional situation provides Honolulu with both an obligation and an opportunity. It is our obligation to our Asian neighbors to assist them in meeting the enormous environmental challenges that confront them. This very situation, however, also presents us with a unique opportunity to market our skills and technology in urban infrastructure development and environmental sustainability and in so doing diversify our economy with knowledge-based industries.

Mayor's Asia-Pacific Environmental Summit

The first step in this process was to earn Honolulu a reputation as a leading global center for urban environmental knowledge and technology. The Mayor's Asia-Pacific Environmental Summit was established in 1999 and soon became recognized as one of the leading urban environmental programs in the world. The Summit brings together mayors and urban leaders from over 100 cities in 30 nations on a biannual basis. The Summit process brings mayors into contact with the world's leading experts in environmental and urban management and technology, forms regional partnerships to deal with urban challenges, and assists leaders in developing plans and strategies to make their cities more sustainable. The Summits, as well as the intervening biannual executive seminars, showcase Hawaii firms with expertise in urban environmental management and technology, and provide opportunities to meet and establish business ties with Asian cities. The goal is to attract national and international firms to our city. Asia's cities should turn to Honolulu when they need technical and scientific expertise, and every international firm hoping to do business with Asian cities should recognize that they need to have an office in Honolulu.

To further our economic development efforts in this area, the City also developed the Asia-Pacific Urban Institute in conjunction with the Board of Water Supply. This facility, located at Kapolei Hale, serves as a training center for local and international urban leaders in environmental technology.

The Asia-Pacific Urban Institute at Kapolei Hale.

View of the Koolau mountains from Haiku Valley.

Chapter 7
The Environment

Island people should have an innate understanding about sustainability. On an island the finite nature of things is self-evident. There is only so much land to build on and cultivate. There is only so much water to drink and irrigate crops. Our forests, valleys, streams and coral reefs are all visibly finite. The limits to growth, perhaps less clear on a continental landmass, are painfully obvious in an island ecosystem.

The need to conserve and recycle resources is vital on an island. These principles were well understood by the ancient Hawaiians. Experts believe that before Western contact, the island of Oahu supported a large population living self sufficiently. The rigid laws and mores embodied in the kapu system served to manage and conserve natural resources. Hawaiian culture was largely a sustainable culture when the first westerners arrived.

Unfortunately, with westernization came the breakdown of the *kapu* system and the *ahupuaa* method of land management. Forests were stripped of sandalwood to satisfy the China trade, wiping out the very tree that these islands were named after. Cultural sites and wildlife habitats were plowed under to open up more acreage for sugar and "pine." Natural streams were diverted and aquatic habitats destroyed to satisfy the unquenchable thirst of the plantation agricultural industry. Competition for limited water resources persists as an environmental issue to this day.

"Wai"

"Wai" is the Hawaiian word for freshwater. Hawaii's indigenous people, the *Kanaka Maoli*, understood the intrinsic value of this precious natural resource. *Kane*, one of Hawaii's greatest gods, is known as the waterfinder, the giver of life.

Hawaiians associated water with prosperity and its use was carefully regulated. Water from the top of the stream was used for drinking, while further down, the water was used for irrigation, and below that, Hawaiians could wash their utensils and calabash. They reserved the bottom of the stream for bathing.

The *Kanaka Maoli* were the first developers and managers of Oahu's water supply. Through careful use of water, they cultivated great areas of land, turning dry lands into productive land by bringing in water from streams and springs through ditches.

The arrival of Captain Cook in 1778 marked the beginning of Hawaii's contact with the West. Oahu's surface and spring water resources were pushed to the limit as new demands were made to accommodate sugar and other crops, cattle ranching, and the new settlers.

One of these settlers, James Campbell, was looking for a source of water for his ranch, which was located on the dry and dusty Ewa Plains. In 1879, Campbell brought in James Ashley, a water driller from California. Ashley erected a drilling rig about a quarter of a mile from the ocean. After weeks of drilling, fresh water came gushing to the surface. Ashley had hit the underground lens, and water history on Oahu was made.

By 1910, there were 430 wells throughout Oahu. The underground water supply seemed limitless. Unregulated, wasteful pumping, however, had a price. Much more water was being taken from the lens than was being returned by rainfall. Clearly, sustainable management of this vital natural resource was needed.

The territorial legislature passed a law in 1929 creating the Board of Water Supply. To this day, the Board continues to be a semi-autonomous city agency, which has the power to develop, manage, and sell our water resources, and plan for Oahu's future water needs.

As a result of careful management and the application of cutting-edge technology, Oahu's potable water resources are now supporting a population of almost a million people, far more than in 1929. To make this system sustainable, however, the City and the Board are implementing a number of innovative conservation and reuse programs.

To understand Oahu's efforts to develop a sustainable water system, it's important to understand the hydrology of the island. Everyday, about two billion gallons of rain fall on Oahu. A third of this water either evaporates or is taken up by plants, and another third runs into streams and catch basins. The rest of the water, almost 670 million gallons a day seeps through the porous volcanic rock into the island's aquifers. In some areas, overlapping lava flows create impenetrable dikes forming compartments in the mountains that trap fresh water. Once tapped, these diked waters flow without the need of pumps because of their high elevation.

Most of the rainwater, however, percolates slowly through the porous basaltic island until it reaches the salt water that has seeped through the island base from the ocean. There the fresh rainwater, having slowly filtered its way through volcanic rock for 25 to 50 years, floats as a lens on the denser salt water.

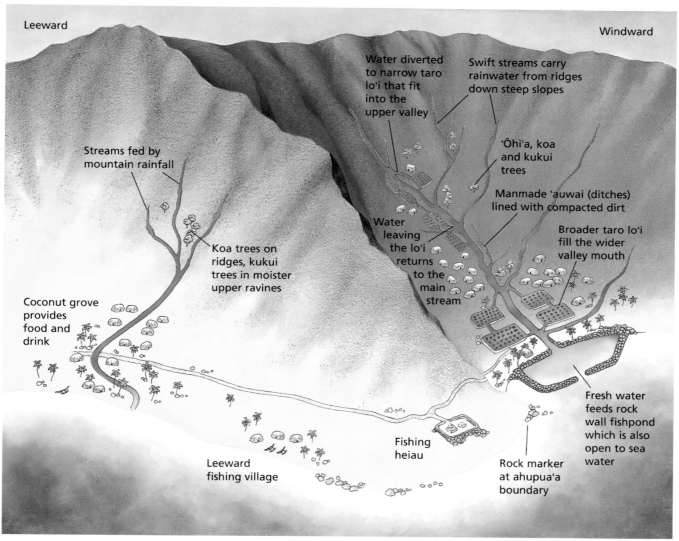

Leeward

Windward

Water diverted to narrow taro lo'i that fit into the upper valley

Swift streams carry rainwater from ridges down steep slopes

Streams fed by mountain rainfall

'Ōhi'a, koa and kukui trees

Manmade 'auwai (ditches) lined with compacted dirt

Koa trees on ridges, kukui trees in moister upper ravines

Water leaving the lo'i returns to the main stream

Broader taro lo'i fill the wider valley mouth

Coconut grove provides food and drink

Fresh water feeds rock wall fishpond which is also open to sea water

Fishing heiau

Leeward fishing village

Rock marker at ahupua'a boundary

Ahupuaa.

As long as the amount of fresh water being pumped out of this lens is less than the amount that is seeping through the rock and recharging the aquifer, the system is sustainable. If too much is pumped, however, the salt water on which the fresh water floats is penetrated and the well becomes salty. Pumping too much and disturbing this halocline – the density boundary between the salt and fresh water – can "break the lens" and destroy the purity of the water source for geologic time. The Board carefully monitors its wells to make sure this never happens, so that our fresh water system will be sustainable in perpetuity.

Conserving our Water

One way to ensure that we don't use more water than is being recharged is to conserve water and reduce consumption and waste. To accomplish this goal, an array of conservation and reuse programs have been established. As a result of these creative initiatives, Oahu's daily water consumption today is 20 million gallons a day less than earlier demand projections.

One of the City's first efforts at water conservation involved a rebate program to encourage property owners to retrofit their buildings with low-flush toilets. Over 68,000 rebates have been issued under this program since its inception, saving almost half a million gallons of water each day.

A further partnership with Hawaiian Electric provides rebates for homeowners who purchase super water and energy efficient washing machines. This landmark agreement also provides for water and energy audits for major consumers.

The Board, the City, and the University of Hawaii have also entered into an agreement to develop water conservation projects on the Manoa Campus. Water audits, low-flow fixture retrofits, sub-metering and an array of non-portable water source development programs are part of that conservation plan.

A wide array of high technology is used in sustainably managing Oahu's water supply. "Supervising Control and Data Acquisition" (SCADA) systems monitor reservoir levels and system pressure. Geographic Information Systems (GIS) compile all the information available about the water system on an interactive computer database. The location, type, and age of over 2,000 miles of pipes, water main break data, development plans—all the data needed to efficiently manage and make strategic decisions about Oahu's complex water system is available on the G.I.S. Water meter telemetry systems signal city computers with water usage data, eliminating the costly and time-consuming door-to-door manual reading of the island's thousands of water meters. And to maintain the purity of our drinking water, Board chemists and microbiologists constantly test the water for chemical contamination, mineral content and bacteria. In localized areas, where agricultural chemicals leaching from the soil have entered the water system, sophisticated filtration systems have been established to remove the contamination.

Technology can only go so far in limiting the waste of our precious water resources. The real recipe for sustainability is to change people's behavior through education. To teach the community about conservation, television and radio spots have been developed featuring local performers and opinion leaders. The annual Detect A Leak program encourages residents to check their homes for costly water leaks, and table tents at local restaurants remind diners that water will only be served on request.

One of the most unique water conservation education programs is designed to reduce the amount of potable water used for irrigation. Fifty percent of the water consumption in the average single-family home goes to outdoor uses, primarily irrigation. To reduce this staggering number, the Board has begun a program to encourage the use of xeriscaping, or the use of low water demanding plants. This simple change in practice reduces a home's outdoor water consumption by between 30 to 80 percent.

Perhaps the most important initiative in our water sustainability program is the recycling and reuse of wastewater.

Managing Our Wastewater

While most people have a fairly good understanding of where our fresh water comes from, very few know or care what happens to the water after it goes down the drain. Yet how we handle our wastewater has a profound impact on the health of our community and our quality of life.

The handling and treatment of sewage is the second most regulated industry in the United States, second only to the nuclear power industry. To meet the stringent requirements of the Federal Clean Water Act, the City has developed an elaborate, high-tech system of wastewater collection and treatment.

The handling of sewage has not always been high tech on Oahu.

Few areas of city management have undergone a more radical transformation in the past hundred years than Honolulu's sewage treatment operations. The city's original sewage system was built around the turn of the 20th century when Honolulu's population was less than 40,000. By today's standards it was primitive, and amounted to little more than a series of clay and cast iron pipes that simply discharged untreated waste into the sea near the entrance of Honolulu Harbor. Cracks in the pipes were patched in piecemeal fashion. So long as the population remained relatively low, the resulting pollution was tolerated.

With the influx of larger numbers of people to Oahu during the Second World War came the gradual realization that if tourism was to be successfully expanded in the post-war era, the City would have to take measures to safeguard the cleanliness and safety of its beaches and recreational waters. Meanwhile, a growing body of evidence suggested the need for the treatment of sewage prior to discharge. By the 1940s it was recommended that bathing and the gathering of *limu* be prohibited in the waters from Fort DeRussy to the southeast point of Sand Island.

Over the next several decades the city's sewer system evolved both in response to and in anticipation of its ever-expanding population. By the 1970s a comparatively sophisticated wastewater collection and treatment system was in place featuring miles of interconnected sewer lines that collected flows from trunk sewers and delivered it to treatment plants for processing.

Today, Honolulu's wastewater treatment is an incredibly complex system of high technology with microbiology laboratories, unmanned submarines, robotic video cameras and sophisticated telemetry systems, all supporting over 2,100 miles of sewer pipes, 65 pump stations and eight treatment plants.

Honolulu's wastewater treatment systems are designed to mimic the natural process of microbial breakdown of organic materials.

SYNAGRO

A Residuals Management Company

Over the last decade, the City has budgeted almost a billion dollars for wastewater treatment upgrades around the island. Under construction at the Sand Island Wastewater Treatment Facility is a cutting-edge ultra violet disinfection facility. Nearby, the new Synagro plant, also under construction, will recycle sewage sludge into a marketable agricultural product.

151

Our treatment plants are biological systems designed to encourage and support nature's handling of waste. The difference is that on its own, nature may take 45 to 60 days to breakdown waste; in our plants we help the natural processes do it in six to ten hours.

To disinfect the treated wastewater, the Honouliuli plant uses cutting edge ultra-violet technology, similar to what's used in an operating room. A similar U.V. disinfection system is currently under construction at the Sand Island Wastewater Treatment Plant.

The reuse of wastewater is a high priority for Honolulu. Every gallon of treated effluent that we can use for agriculture or industry is one less gallon of potable water we need for those purposes.

To provide irrigation water for the Ewa Plain and industrial water for industries at Campbell Industrial Park, the City, in partnership with U.S. Filter, developed a 12 million gallon a day wastewater recycling plant at Honouliuli. The state of the art plant, one of the most advanced in the United States, takes secondarily treated sewage effluent and "polishes" it so the water is clean and safe and can be used to irrigate golf courses and cool industrial plants.

Currently, all of the solids that are removed from the sewage are treated, dried and dumped in the landfill. That will change in the near future with the completion of the City's new Synagro plant. This new facility will take this processed waste and further treat it, transforming it into a valuable soil amendment.

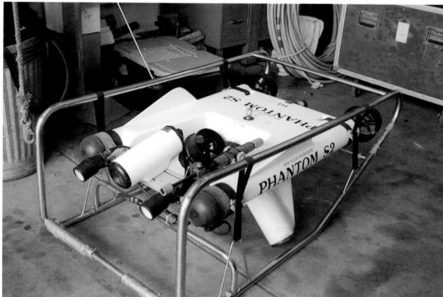

Ultra violet disinfection for wastewater recycling, robotic video cameras for sewer line monitoring, and remote controlled unmanned submarines for deep ocean outfall inspection typify Honolulu's high-tech approach to wastewater treatment.

This will lessen the City's need for landfill space and convert what was once an environmental liability into an asset. The City has processed solids into compost from Honouliuli since 1998 in partnership with the Navy.

In 1995 the City entered into an agreement with the EPA on a 20-year plan for major upgrades to the island's wastewater treatment system. Over the last ten years, the City has budgeted approximately $900 million for these improvements and is on schedule with the EPA upgrade plan.

The difficulty with the City's sewer system deals with the 2,100 miles of sewer pipes which crisscross the island and the thousands of miles of sewer laterals, which run from private homes to the street. The problem is known as "I and I," which stands for inflow and infiltration. On our unstable island, with expanding and slumping soils, sewer lines shift and crack. Since these lines aren't pressurized, sewage doesn't leak out, but during flooding conditions, rainwater leaks into the sewer pipes. During large storms, millions of gallons of rainwater leak into our system and end up at our treatment plants, overwhelming them. The portion of this floodwater that cannot be handled by the plant is sent out the deep ocean outfall with minimal treatment.

The only solution to this problem is to dig up the streets and replace and repair lines that are allowing rainwater to leak in. This is extremely expensive and disruptive to traffic and road maintenance. Many streets on the island that are in need of resurfacing are streets that are slated for this type of underground utility work.

Since it would waste millions of tax dollars repairing streets only to dig them up again, the City has deferred resurfacing on these streets until the underground utility work is done.

One of our largest inflow and infiltration problems, however, doesn't deal with city sewer pipes, but with the privately owned pipes in people's yards. Studies have shown that an enormous amount of the rainwater that infiltrates our sewer system comes from this source.

To solve this problem, homeowners would have to spend thousands of dollars of their own money digging up their yards and replacing their sewer connection laterals. The City is trying to avoid this by expanding the sewage treatment plant to be able to handle the millions of gallons of rainwater that reach the plant from people's yards during large storms.

Storm Water

It may come as a surprise that sewage spills are not the main cause of water pollution problems on Oahu. Water pollution is mainly caused by polluted runoff. Pollutants such as the used oil poured down the gutter and the pesticides over-applied to lawns, all wash into the nearest stream during rains. This untreated storm water pollutes stream and coastal waters. Since everyone is responsible for creating this non-point source pollution, it can only be stopped if everyone plays their part.

Storm drain stenciling, recycling and community educational programs throughout Oahu help protect Honolulu's environment, November 2000, Bruce Asato (The Honolulu Advertiser).

To teach the community about solving this problem, the City has mounted an extensive public education campaign. Television spots featuring celebrities teach people about runoff, and community volunteers stencil storm drains, letting people know that whatever is thrown into the catch basin goes directly to the stream. Workshops and presentations to businesses and industry groups on best management practices are also part of the outreach effort to reduce pollution.

Adopt-a-Stream programs have involved community groups and businesses in the care and cleaning of streams running through their neighborhoods, and thousands of young Earth Protection Agents have been trained and certified to look for environmental violations in their communities and report them to authorities. Enforcement against violators is an important component of the storm water program.

Keeping our island waters clean requires all of us to be more environmentally conscious and more involved in our community.

Solid Waste/Recycling

For most of the 20th century, refuse on Oahu was simply left at the local dump, or in later years burned at incinerators around the island. This practice polluted the air with poisonous gases, tainted our waters with leachate runoff, and filled our valleys with garbage. A more sustainable method to handle the island's refuse was obviously needed.

Today, the Waimanalo Gulch sanitary landfill in Nanakuli is the only operational landfill on Oahu for general and municipal solid waste (MSW). Owned by the City, it is operated by Waste Management of Hawaii, a privately owned company.

Unlike years past, today's landfills are no longer simply dumps. State of the art liners and drainage plumbing systems are installed under the landfill to protect the groundwater and soil from pollution.

A major step toward sustainability was made in 1989 with the establishment of the Honolulu Program of Waste Energy Recovery, or H-POWER. H-POWER was designed and built with the goal of turning Honolulu's refuse into energy, thereby reducing the volume of refuse by turning it into ash.

Built at a cost of $181 million, this waste-to-energy facility has disposed of over 8,450,000 tons of municipal solid waste or MSW since it began operations.

To get an idea of how much garbage that is, picture an area the size of a football stadium— 8.45 million tons of rubbish would fill the football stadium and rise almost four and a quarter miles into the air.

H-POWER recycles the metals out of the refuse and then turns the rest into a fuel, which it burns to generate electricity. In so doing, the volume of refuse is reduced by 90 percent.

The H-Power waste to energy power plant converts over 2,000 tons of waste per day, reducing Oahu's need for imported fossil fuels.

H-POWER turns refuse into recyclable metals, electricity and ash. That ash now goes to a special landfill that is only for ash, a monofill, at Waimanalo Gulch. The City's goal is to recycle the ash from H-POWER by turning it into asphalt—using it to repave city roads.

H-POWER operates 24-hours a day, seven days a week. The plant was designed to process 561,600 tons of refuse a year. Since the plant started operating, it has processed on average 607,000 tons a year. When H-POWER is shutdown for maintenance, the refuse has to be diverted to the landfill. To solve this problem, the City is moving ahead with the development of a third boiler at H-Power so it can operate through maintenance periods without interruption. The plant works by processing the waste into an efficient fuel before it is burned. It's called "Refuse Derived Fuel" or "RDF."

In fiscal year 2003, H-POWER generated nearly 338 million watts of electricity, which it sold to Hawaiian Electric for $30 million. That's enough electricity to power about 60,000 households.

In terms of the amount of fossil fuel saved, it would take 66 gallons of oil to produce the same amount of energy H-POWER produces with every ton of municipal solid waste it burns. In its 14 years of service, H-Power has eliminated the need to import about 510 million gallons of oil to Honolulu.

In addition to reducing the amount of waste that ends up in the landfill and generating waste-to-energy electricity, there is a third key component to H-POWER: recycling.

Magnets in its pre-processing system pull out iron and steel before they get to the boiler. Nonferrous metal — primarily aluminum — is extracted from the ash after the refuse-derived fuel has been burned. This means virtually 100 percent of ferrous and nonferrous metals entering H-POWER are recycled.

Recycling as much solid waste as possible is vital to keeping our island home sustainable. In your home, about 15 percent of your trash is recyclable newspaper, aluminum, glass and plastic. Another 25 to 30 percent is compostable yard waste. The type of recyclable materials found at work depends on the business. In the average office, for example, as much as 85 percent of what gets tossed out is recyclable office paper.

A new state law called "Beverage Container Deposit System," or the "Bottle Bill" for short, will further enhance our recycling efforts. Beginning in 2005, there will be a nickel deposit on beverage containers, which you pay when you buy the beverage. You'll be able to get your deposit back when you return the empties to the store or a redemption center.

The container deposit system is further complemented by the City's new curbside recycling program, which will provide residents living in single-family homes with the additional convenience of curbside pickup. The project aims to further increase recycling rates throughout the island, and is scheduled to be fully operational island-wide by mid 2005.

The City provides a number of other services, such as bulky item pickup, to make it easier for people to recycle and dispose of large items. Yard waste is collected by city crews and turned into mulch and compost and sold locally.

The City also plans on building an alternative technology-recycling park adjacent to H-POWER. The City will provide the land and encourage private recycling companies to locate there, utilizing new technologies to recycle city waste.

Through stepped up recycling efforts, the expansion of H-POWER, a new sorting center, and the employment of new technologies, the City hopes to be able to greatly reduce the need for a landfill. In the meantime, the City has pledged to close the Waimanalo Gulch MSW landfill within five years.

Ultimately, however, solid waste problems cannot be addressed with technology alone. The true solution is for people to realize that we cannot continue to consume resources and generate waste as we have in the past. We need to focus on waste reduction instead of waste handling.

From the way we package products to the type of bags we use to bring groceries home from the store, our society needs to shift to a new paradigm, a new way of thinking.

The old idea of throwing garbage away is a thing of the past. There is no such thing as "garbage" and there is no such thing as "away." Solid waste is just another natural resource waiting to be reused.

Biodiversity and Invasive Species

Hawaii has the dubious distinction of being the "extinction capital" of the world. More species have gone extinct or are threatened with extinction in these islands than anywhere else on the planet. One of the greatest assaults on Oahu's native ecosystems has been the introduction of invasive species. From wild pigs, to mongoose and myconia, over the last century, hundreds of non-native species have been brought to these islands. In almost every case, environmental damage has resulted.

Oahu's largest lake, Lake Wilson, was choked by an invasive aquatic plant, _Salvinia molesta_, illustrating the island's vulnerability to invasive exotic species.

The most notable example of this assault was the strangling of Lake Wilson with the aggressive aquarium plant _Salvinia molesta_. One plant in the ideal growing conditions of the lake turned into hundreds of millions of plants in a matter of months, choking the lake and threatening the fish population. Only the use of cutting-edge aquatic excavation technology and the expenditure of millions of dollars by the City cleared the lake before an environmental disaster occurred. The warning was clear, however, unless we fiercely protect our island from the importation of non-endemic plant and animal species, Oahu's unique biodiversity will be threatened.

Chapter 8
Quality of Life

There is more to the quality of life in a city than sewers and sidewalks. A vibrant, livable city is characterized by culture and arts, parks and recreational facilities, beautiful streets and safe neighborhoods. These qualities are equally important to the economy of cities, as well. In today's tourism marketplace, a city has to be a great place to live in order to be a great city to visit. But the quality of life in a city affects its economy in more ways than just tourism. Over the next 10 to 15 years, for every two workers from the Baby Boomer generation that retire, only one Generation X worker will be available to fill the void. Unlike their predecessors, this new generation is not moving to cities in search of jobs. Instead, members of Generation X are choosing where they live based on quality of life issues. They are moving to exciting, vibrant cities that have great amenities and a variety of things to do.

Featured at the Aloha Friday Hawaiian Concert Series are *Halau Na Mamo `O Pu`uanahulu kupuna* (elders), 2004 Miss *Keiki Hula*, 2003 Miss *Aloha Hula* Jennifer Oyama and her hula sisters under the direction of *Kumu Hula* Sonny Ching, and the women of *Halau Hula `O Hokulani*.

Aloha Friday Hawaiian Concerts at the newly restored historic Mission Memorial Auditorium feature Merrie Monarch and Na Hoku Hanohano award winners Roy Sakuma and his ukulele Super Kids and 2003 Miss Aloha Hula Jennifer Oyama, Halau Na Mamo `O Pu`uanahulu. The Galliard String Quartet of the Honolulu Symphony has also performed.

Honolulu City Lights, the premier Christmas festival, has delighted hundreds of thousands of residents and visitors for 20 years.

In the 21st century, companies and jobs are following the most talented workers.

So the message is clear, if a city wants to be competitive in today's world for tourists or talent, it must provide a high quality of life.

Parks

Urban planner Charles Mulford Robinson's dream a century ago to make Honolulu "one of the most beautiful cities in the world—all one great park, with a city tucked in between," has never been fully realized.

The establishment of major parks at Kapiolani and Ala Moana, and the banning of billboards by the Outdoor Circle, were all major steps in protecting the beauty of Honolulu. But the chance for the world class "park city" that Robinson envisioned was largely squandered. Opportunities for good urban design with green belts and mauka-makai view plains with pedestrian pathways were over-ridden by a powerful real estate development lobby. Profit, not planning, drove Honolulu's growth through most of the 20th century and the grand opportunity was lost.

Instead of becoming a city nestled in a park, Honolulu had to settle for parks shoehorned into a sprawling city.

With the rapid population growth in the 1960s and 70s, the squeeze on park and recreational facilities intensified. The Park Dedication Ordinance, which required developers to provide land or money for parks in new developments helped somewhat, but by the mid 1980s soccer fields, baseball fields, pools and tennis courts were all inadequate to serve the needs of our growing community. Drugs and gangs in Honolulu were on the rise at the same time, and City recreational facilities strained to meet the needs of our youth.

Despite the recession and the precipitous drop in city real property tax revenue in the 1990s, the decision was made to invest in a major expansion of parks and recreational facilities to meet this vital need. Many of the new recreational facilities, such as the Waipio Soccer Complex and the Central Oahu Regional Park were designed to bring in sports tourism revenue as well as provide first class athletic facilities for Honolulu's families. A host of other projects were also developed to meet additional long-standing needs, as well.

Outrigger canoe paddling, the signature sport of the islands, had been shamefully ignored for decades. Despite the fact that thousands of Oahu's citizens are involved in this culturally important recreational activity, few facilities were provided by the City. To remedy this situation, new canoe *halau* were built at Kailua, Hawaii Kai, Kewalo Basin and Waimanalo, and still others are nearing construction or in design at Pokai Bay, Makaha, Kahaluu, Ala Moana, Nanakuli and Haleiwa.

The 269-acre Central Oahu Regional Park includes softball, baseball, archery, soccer, rugby, tennis and soon to be completed world-class swimming and diving facilities unmatched in the United States.

The Pinky Thompson Canoe Halau and Pohaku, dedicated in August 2002.

New swimming pools have been developed around the island, ending a twenty-year moratorium that left many youngsters without basic water safety skills.

Many of Oahu's young people are also involved in skateboarding, but again, almost no facilities were available for this increasingly popular sport. Left without properly designed skate parks, skaters practiced their hobby in dangerous drainage ditches and at commercial private property sites. As an object lesson in democracy, young skaters brought this problem to the city administration's attention, and then worked with Parks Department engineers to plan and design skate facilities around the island. Their volunteer participation and hard work led to the construction of new skate board facilities at Kahuku, Kamilo Iki, Kaneohe, Kailua, Makiki and Mililani, and in-line skating hockey rinks at Kamilo Iki, Kaneohe and Kaomaaiku.

No Swimming

Throughout the 1970s, 80s and the first half of the 90s, the City had a moratorium on swimming pool construction. Pools were viewed as a luxury, not a necessity, and as a result, no new city pools were developed as the City's population grew. As a result of this shortsighted policy, an alarmingly high percentage of Honolulu's young people never learned how to swim.

If you live on an island, learning to swim is a necessity not a luxury, and more needed to be done to provide venues for aquatic instruction. In response, new pool facilities were constructed in Makiki and Salt Lake, and a world-class aquatic and dive complex was developed in Central Oahu to address this need.

Building for Kids

Demand for additional indoor recreational facilities was met with the development of new gymnasiums in Manoa, Waipahu, and Waimanalo, while older facilities were upgraded at various locations around the island. And with the support of the police, controversial late night basketball leagues were established at selective sites to provide at-risk teenagers with a nighttime alternative to gang activity.

For those youngsters who are less athletic, the Computers in the Parks program was started. At 14 regional parks around the island, computer centers were established providing computers with free Internet access. New city web sites for kids and the elderly were developed to help with homework and access service programs. Playgrounds for young children were woefully inadequate for a population the size of Honolulu's. This problem was exacerbated when the State demolished aging playgrounds at schools around the island, because of safety concerns. Faced with the prospect of an entire generation of children growing up without access to slides or jungle gyms, the City responded, and installed 79 new, safe play apparatus around the island.

Parks for the Future

In recent years, the island's parkland has grown faster than at any time in the City's history. Nearly 4,000 acres of new parks were developed around the island, increasing the city's park inventory by 65 percent.

The Waianae Coast, long ignored for improvement, saw the development of the three-mile long Ulehawa Beach Park and the Mauna Lahilahi Shoreline Park.

Along the Windward side, hundreds of acres of additional parkland were acquired at Heeia Kea, Kahaluu, Waiahole, and Waikane Valley. Older parks along this coast were revitalized, and a new district park was constructed in Kahaluu.

On the North Shore new beach park improvements were made at Pupukea and Sunset, and the 1,798-acre Waimea Falls Park was acquired as a nature-learning center.

In the Ewa area, the West Loch Shoreline Park and West Loch Peninsula were developed. Two new city golf courses were built at Honouliuli and Ewa Village, and several new community parks were created in Kapolei, Ewa and Manana to provide citizens in this growing area of the island with recreational opportunities.

Even in the densely developed downtown area, new park facilities blossomed forth. Aala Park was transformed from a homeless refuge to a community-gathering place, the new Smith-Beretania Park was created and Fort Street Mall was revitalized and re-landscaped.

Kahaluu District Park and the Waiahole/Waikane Coastline. Over the last ten years, almost 4,000 acres have been added to Honolulu's park system.

Park Expansion. The City has acquired hundreds of acres of waterfront land for park expansion along the Windward coast.

Park Expansion. The Heeia Kea lands above the small boat harbor were added to the City's park inventory and the 1,798-acre Waimea Falls Park was acquired as a nature learning center operated by the Audubon Society.

In every area of the island, new neighborhood and community parks emerged and Charles Robinson's vision of making Honolulu one of the most beautiful cities in the world became more of a reality.

Beautifying Paradise

Honolulu's renaissance has also been characterized by the beautification of the island's roadways and neighborhoods and the reforesting of the City. Thousands of mature trees have been planted throughout Honolulu. Gateway points into the City, such as the Pali Highway, Punchbowl Street, and Ala Moana Boulevard, were transformed from ugly traffic corridors to lovely tree canopied greenbelts under the spreading boughs of monkeypod trees.

Chinatown sidewalks were repaved with granite pavers reminiscent of historic sailing ship ballast blocks, and the streets were lined with vibrant green fiddlewood trees. Every community on the island, from Kalihi to Hawaii Kai saw the greening of its streets and the beautification of its neighborhoods. Today, the City's Division of Urban Forestry maintains more than 236,000 trees throughout our City, and we have earned the proud distinction of "Tree City USA."

Public art also adds to the quality of urban life on the island. Bronze sculptures, both whimsical and historical grace our city streets and parks, and lovely water features in Chinatown, Downtown and Waikiki have earned Honolulu the nickname, "the City of Waterfalls."

Chinatown Historic District Renaissance. Sidewalks repaired with granite pavers reminiscent of historic sailing ship ballast blocks and streets lined with fiddlewood trees were part of the revitalization of Honolulu's Historic District.

Implementing the Vision. Pali Highway, a major gateway to Downtown Honolulu, was transformed into a tree-canopied greenbelt.

184

Roadside Beautification. Through the years, beautification along the roadways around the island has improved the quality of life in Honolulu. Mahogany trees planted on Kalakaua Avenue between King and McCully Street by the Outdoor Circle, Circa 1917 (Hawaii State Archives).

Safety and Security

One of the cornerstones of a livable and sustainable community is safety and security. People need to feel safe walking down the street in the evening. Visitors need to feel secure and protected from terrorism or attack.

Through the 1960s and 70s, Honolulu's Police Department often felt like the orphan child of the City. Located in the old Sears and Roebuck building in Pawaa, HPD's main headquarters was woefully inadequate. The City's ballistic testing facility consisted of a cardboard box in an old clothes closet.

Despite a significant decline in property tax revenues in the 1990s, Honolulu developed stronger police, fire and emergency response capabilities than at any time in its history and made major investments in public safety technology, facilities, equipment and personnel.

In 1994 crime statistics skyrocketed. Property crime and violent crime seemed out of control to the point that the Japanese Consul General considered warning prospective visitors from Japan that it was unsafe to travel to Honolulu. In response to the problem, the police force was expanded and better equipped. Over 433 police officers were added to the force, and new police facilities were built around the island. A new regional police station was developed in Kapolei and new "storefront" police facilities were developed in a number of communities.

Honolulu's Public Safety Program. The last decade has seen a tremendous expansion of Police, Fire and Emergency Services facilities around the island.

Honolulu's Finest. As a result of increased staffing, training, technology and facilities, Honolulu's Police and Fire departments have been recognized as among the best in the nation. Bottom: Honolulu Police Chief Boisse Correa and officers in personal protective equipment, Deborah Booker, The Honolulu Advertiser, February 2003.

Honolulu Fire Department. Top Left: Bishop Street Fire, June 2003 (David Yamada, The Honolulu Advertiser). Fire boat Mokuahi. Chief Attillio Leonardi (right) and Deputy Chief John Clark (left) and the Honolulu Fire Department Honor Guard. Bottom Right: Horse-drawn fire truck, Circa 1922 (R.J. Baker, Hawaii State Archives).

The expansion of personnel and facilities was matched with an investment in technology. New communication systems, fingerprint computers and a DNA laboratory brought the department into the 21st century. In 2003 the Honolulu Police Department became one of only 14 major departments in the country to be accredited by the commission on accreditation for Law Enforcement Agencies, and Honolulu was rated one of the safest cities in the nation.

The expansion and improvement of Honolulu Fire Department facilities and preparedness has been no less impressive over this time period. During that time the number of firefighters was increased and a number of fire stations were built, replaced and renovated. The department also developed one of the most extensive HAZMAT response programs in the country enabling the City to respond to hazardous materials spills or the deployment of chemical or biological weapons. From infrared scopes that allow firefighters to see through thick smoke to NOTAR helicopters with heat sensory telemetry systems to find lost hikers in heavy underbrush, HFD went high tech. The result of these investments was the accreditation of the department by the Commission on Fire Accreditation International. At the time, only 34 of 32,000 fire departments in America had been so designated.

One of the City's greatest advances in safety and security was in the area of homeland security. In 1997, four years before the attacks of September 11, 2001, Honolulu was one of the first cities in the nation to develop a Terrorism Emergency Response Plan.

With the Department of Emergency Services taking the lead, Honolulu became one of the leading cities in the nation in developing technology and procedures to deal with terrorism. The City developed the capability to monitor 12 separate community events simultaneously for the release of biological weapons, with mobile, hand held field-testing equipment. If a biological weapon, such as anthrax, is detected by this field-testing technology, the City is capable of immediately dispatching a mobile DNA laboratory to the site to do a definitive DNA test on the sample. If the agent is verified as anthrax, the city has the mobile capability to deliver and distribute prophylactic antibiotic to more than 100,000 people.

In addition to this mobile monitoring capability, Honolulu has also developed fixed air sampling stations around the City that continuously monitor the air for the release of possible biological weapons. Once again, if such a release is detected, it can be verified, its source located, and the exposed population treated before any outbreak occurs. All of these measures have made our community safer than ever before.

For a city to be sustainable, both economically and environmentally, it must have a good quality of life. High quality of life cities all possess certain characteristics—parks, culture, arts, good urban design and safe streets. Over the last 100 years, Honolulu has been evolving through many stage of sustainability. Its renaissance has made it one of the truly great cosmopolitan cities of the world.

Vision for Kakaako. Blighted areas of Honolulu can be transformed into vibrant places to live, work and play with good planning and citizen involvement.

Chapter 9
Vision for the Future

Honolulu's development over the last century has been largely unplanned and driven by forces outside our control. As we enter the new century—the Asia-Pacific Century, the Urban Century—it's important that we take control of our own destiny. Our future needs to be one of our own choosing, based on the values of our community and the vision of our people.

This is a special time in our City's history. It is a time to look within ourselves and ask questions about who we are as individuals and who we are collectively. It is a time for us to set our sights on the future we want for ourselves, our island, and our children. The world itself is at a turning point. Human civilization will either continue on its current path of ever-accelerating resource consumption and waste generation, or we will adopt a sustainable relationship with this planet that will allow us to persevere.

The 21st Century Vision Process. The Vision Process empowered people to develop sustainable plans for the future of their neighborhoods, their community, and their island.

Our fate will be decided by our cities and whether they can adapt and manage themselves sustainably. Honolulu has the potential to become a model for the world in this regard. The world already recognizes Honolulu as a great city. Now is the time for us to rededicate ourselves to making our great city a model for a sustainable future.

Looking back, the changes that have occurred on our island over the last 100 years have been extraordinary. We have evolved from an agricultural community with a plantation economy to the 12th largest city in the United States and a center of international tourism. Though these changes have been enormous, they pale in comparison to the changes that await us in the years ahead. We face immense challenges, to be sure, but make no mistake: our future is one of great hope and opportunity if we have the vision, courage, and initiative to seize it. To realize this opportunity we need a shared vision for our island's future and that vision must be sustainable.

Over the last six years, we have worked to empower the people of this island to be active participants in creating and realizing that shared vision. Through the 21st Century Vision Process, we have empowered people to develop sustainable plans for the future of their neighborhoods, their community, and their island.

The results of this experiment in grass roots democracy have been remarkable. The program yielded stunning successes and disappointing defeats, but what emerged from the messy democratic process was a new community-based vision for the future of Honolulu, that revolved around several main themes.

Keep The Country, Country

The first theme to emerge from the visioning process dealt with land use. The continuing spread of urban sprawl across our open space and agricultural lands must stop. We must end the practice of developing bedroom communities separated from places of work and school. New "smart growth" principles need to be implemented that use mixed use zoning and other land use planning techniques to create communities that are not built around the car, but around the people. The slogan that has come to embody this theme and these concepts is "keep the country, country."

To accomplish this vision, we need to redirect future growth on the island to our primary urban center in Honolulu and to the second city of Kapolei. To visualize the change that will result from these new urban design and land use practices, the vision process developed digital images of the transformation that could occur in Kapolei. They illustrate how an urban area built around the automobile can be transformed into a people-oriented sustainable community.

In addition to redirecting future growth to the two urban centers, a key component of the vision calls for strengthening the sense of place and community in Oahu's rural towns and neighborhoods.

The vision for the future that emerged from the community planning process called for keeping the country, country and reclaiming the island's waterfront from poorly planned development.

The revitalization of the Wahiawa Botanical Gardens, the reconstruction of the bandstand as the new heart of Waialua town, and the planning for a sustainable Waianae ahupuaa, are all examples of this vision. Providing outdoor recreational activities in rural areas is also part of this effort to keep the country, country. The planned greenbelt and bikeway along the North Shore and the suggested equestrian trail through Kipapa Gulch are examples of proposed projects to accomplish this goal.

Another critical component of the land use vision for Oahu was the development of sustainable community plans for rural areas. These plans, which establish urban growth boundaries and protect open space, are instrumental to bringing the community's vision to fruition.

Rebuilding Oahu's communities around people instead of cars requires a different approach to transportation. The Trans 2-K portion of the vision process envisions an expanded bus system reconfigured into a hub-and-spoke network to better serve neighborhoods, the development of a high-capacity hybrid electric bus rapid transit system to move people efficiently to downtown, the building of a network of bikeways to encourage non-automobile travel, and the construction of traffic calming measures to discourage speeding in residential areas.

Many of the programs and projects that are needed to keep the country, country are underway, but much more must be done.

Neighborhood Visions. Revitalizing Kalihi by beautifying King Street (top); transforming Kipapa Glunch into equestrian and hiking trails (second from top); recapturing the waterfront by developing the Pearl Harbor Historic Trail (third from top); and preserving the rural nature of the North Shore with greenbelts (bottom), were all visions for the future that emerged from the planning process.

Protecting The Environment

A second major theme of the community's vision for the island centers around protecting the environment. Recycling the island's waste, shifting to renewable energy, beautifying our roadways, and expanding park facilities, were all seen as important components of our environmental future. To start carrying out the plan, new parks for our young people were developed around the island. Canoe halau, in-line hockey rinks, district park facilities and playgrounds were built.

Beautification projects planted thousands of trees in neighborhoods and along roadways around the island, and ugly arterials like the Pali Highway were transformed into environmental assets.

In addition to beautifying our island, major initiatives were implemented to set the City on a sustainable environmental path. To reduce our reliance on fossil fuels, city facilities were upgraded with energy efficiency systems, city vehicles were converted to biodiesel fuels, and co-generation power plants were developed.

The community also spoke out loudly for recycling. Continuing to fill our valleys with solid waste simply is not sustainable or acceptable. After many unnecessary delays and a successful pilot curbside recycling project in Mililani, the initiation of the City's islandwide curbside recycling is ready to begin.

Neighborhood Visions.   Beautifying neighborhoods and improving parks is a common theme in many communities.

Revitalizing of Neighborhoods

The revitalization of the island's neighborhoods emerged as another important part of the community vision for Oahu. The goal is to recapture the unique history and sense of place of each neighborhood and reverse the trend of homogenization and strip development that has occurred over the last 50 years. Kailua town was transformed with tree-lined medians and urban design improvements. The commercial center at the "Top of the Hill" in Kaimuki was revitalized with parking bays and landscaping, and King Street through Kalihi was renewed as a tree-lined boulevard with historic lighting fixtures.

Chinatown was one of the neighborhoods most transformed. Stone sidewalk pavers, entry gates, cultural signage, historic lights, landscaping, park improvements and a new police station and community center were all part of the vision of a restored historic district. Now even safer than Waikiki, Chinatown has emerged as a great place to live, shop and dine.

Digital images were also developed for other neighborhoods to illustrate the vision of what they could become with appropriate changes in urban design and planning.

These images illustrate how communities such as Pearl City and Liliha could be transformed from automobile-focused thoroughfares to residential neighborhoods.

Revitalizing Neighborhoods. Architectural guidelines, landscape requirements, and new design codes transform neighborhoods and make them more livable.

Revitalizing Neighborhoods. The Pearl City and Aiea corridor can be revitalized with landscaping, bikeways and pedestrian improvements.

Revitalizing Neighborhoods. With good design and streetscape, the intersection of Piikoi and Rycroft streets could have transformed into an exciting commercial and residential district.

Existing Commercial   Local's Dining   'Portmana Pavilion + Food Court   Kalakaua Ave.

Revitalizing Neighborhoods. The area across from the Convention Center could be redeveloped into a town square with commercial shops and outdoor restaurants.

Revitalizing Neighborhoods. The community's vision for Waianae town.

Revitalizing Neighborhoods. Kaimuki's commercial district has been improved with landscaping, parking bays, and sidewalk improvements as a result of community vision. Top Left: Circa 1955 (C. Rosen, Bishop Museum).

Recapturing the Waterfront

As Oahu urbanized over the last 100 years, it turned its back to the water. Beautiful stretches of coastline were scarred by warehouses, strip commercial development and industry. Downtown Honolulu was cut off from its waterfront when its most valuable land was turned into the nine-lane Nimitz Highway. The island's most important resource, its shoreline, was neglected and abused. The vision for Oahu's future calls for the waterfront to be rediscovered and redeveloped.

In Downtown, the plan calls for rerouting Waikiki-bound traffic over a landscaped Sand Island Boulevard and through a tunnel under the mouth of Honolulu Harbor. This would allow Nimitz Highway coming into town to be narrowed and landscaped, shielding out the ugly industrial buildings that welcome people to our tourist destination. Through Downtown, seven lanes of Nimitz Highway could be eliminated and turned into waterfront shops and restaurants with parks and apartments overlooking the water. Honolulu could be transformed into a true waterfront city.

The industrial junkyards that line the shore of Keehi Lagoon behind Sand Island Access Road would be redeveloped into marinas and waterfront recreation facilities under this plan.

The vision of recapturing the waterfront extends to Pearl Harbor as well. The Pearl Harbor Historic Trail project envisions transforming the makai side of Kamehameha Highway from Aiea through Waipahu into a waterfront historic trail.

Recapturing the Waterfront. Honolulu's downtown waterfront could be transformed into parks, bikeways, shops, and restaurants, by rerouting Nimitz Highway over Sand Island and through a tunnel under the entrance to Honolulu Harbor.

Recapturing the Waterfront. The access to Sand Island could become a beautifully landscaped parkway overlooking waterfront parks and marinas.

The old OR&L railroad would be re-established and large areas of harbor frontage would be opened up for parks and view plains to the sea. Waterfront commercial shops and restaurants would be developed in nodes under this plan and oriented to the water. The historic train would carry tourists and locals along this beautiful renewed coast and help strengthen the economy of the entire area.

The plan also calls for the OR&L train to run through Ewa Villages, past the hotels at Ihilani and up the coast to Waianae, sparking an economic resurgence for Leeward communities.

The vision for waterfront revitalization didn't stop there. Plans also call for reorienting Wahiawa around the beautiful Lake Wilson and creating waterfront dining opportunities along the Ala Wai canal. The VFW site across from the Convention Center would be turned into a small marina for canoes and rowboats and a village for making and selling Hawaiian handicrafts would surround the water. A Hawaiian style restaurant on the dock overlooking the boats would allow diners to enjoy a waterfront experience.

At the other end of the Ala Wai, where the library now stands, a beautiful outrigger canoe and surfing museum would be built. With docks and an outdoor restaurant on the water, this would be the focal point of the Ala Wai's sporting and cultural events. Outrigger canoe races, rowing regattas, and the Toro Nagashi floating lantern ceremony could all find their home at this lovely location.

Creative Community Ideas. From recreational improvements along the Kapalama Canal to reinstating the historic OR&L railroad along the Waianae Coast shoreline, creative ideas have emerged from the community to improve the economy and the quality of life on Oahu.

Recapturing the Waterfront. The old VFW site across the Convention Center could be redeveloped into a small marina for canoes and rowboats, with outdoor dining and local handicraft shops.

Recapturing the Waterfront. The Diamond Head end of Ala Wai Canal offers potential for developing a beautiful outrigger canoe and surfing museum with docks, outrigger canoe facilities, and an outdoor restaurant on the water.

Dillingham Shopping Center (now and envisioned). The vision process looks at how Honolulu's neighborhoods can be transformed with good urban design.

Mentioned here are just a few of the themes and the hundreds of ideas and initiatives that were developed by the community through the vision process. The themes and projects that emerged from this process will continue to guide and shape the island for years to come. But the greatest significance of this grand experiment in grassroots democracy cannot be measured in brick and mortar. The real legacy of the 21st Century Vision for Oahu is an empowered citizenry, knowledgeable about sustainability, and dedicated to improving the quality of life on this island.

Postscript

Our islands today are in a time of transition. Our major industries are changing. Sugar, once the economic life blood of this island, is no more. Military spending is uncertain, and our visitor industry faces stiff international competition and calls out for revitalization and redefinition.

Times of transition such as we face today occur infrequently in history. When they do, they are times of risk, uncertainty and challenge, but they also present wonderful opportunities to develop new paradigms and take bold new approaches.

We must seize this historic opportunity to strike out boldly, pursuing our dreams, following our values, and reaching out for our destiny. We have developed an exciting vision for this island. We need to aggressively pursue this vision for the future and renew our commitment to community values. The decisions we make in the next few years will impact the nature of our community and the quality of life in Hawaii for a century to come.

Just as the actions of the 1800s led to the development of the sugar industry, molded our economy, established our cultural diversity, and impacted our land, water and environment for a century, so too will the new course we are setting today shape this island and our society's future.

This new course is a journey to sustainability. Our island has an opportunity and an obligation to become a model for the world for how human civilization can establish a sustainable relationship with this planet. The roots of Hawaiian heritage are firmly anchored in these values. The ancient ethos of this land must be reborn and shared with the world.

The course we have chartered for Honolulu represents the renaissance of a great city and a return to the environmental ethics of our past. This journey to sustainability and world leadership will not be easy, nor will the path always be clear. We will need a compass to steer by, a standard by which we can evaluate our progress. That compass must be our values.

What is truly important to us? What do we hold sacred? What are we unwilling to sacrifice on the alter of economic development or political expediency? I suggest that some of the guiding values are these:

First, we have an obligation to our descendants to take care of this sacred place. We have to care for our land, and we have to protect our environment. We need homes for our families, but we can't sacrifice all of our open space. We need jobs for our people, but we can't overwhelm our coastlines with hotels. A hundred years from now, our children's children should still be able to catch *oopu* in the mountain streams or pick *limu* from the reefs of Ewa. These are values that should not be sacrificed or incrementally dwindled away.

Second, we have an obligation to give our children the love and resources they need, and to sacrifice for them so that their quality of life can be richer, not poorer than our own. No child in Hawaii should ever want for a park to play in or clean air to breath or pure water to drink.

Third, we have an obligation to care for and respect one another. What makes Hawaii great is not just our climate and our natural beauty, but the inner beauty of our people. That which we call the *Aloha Spirit* is alive and real and is a description of a loving, caring, people. Those values should never be sacrificed at any price.

Finally, we have an obligation to the rest of the world to be both model and teacher for a new paradigm for human civilization, a new way of living that is no longer based on consumption and waste, but is grounded in the ethics of conservation and re-issue.

With the pace of technological change in the world today, it is difficult to predict with certainty what the lives of our children and our children's children will be like on this island 100 years from now. But while we may not be able to envision the technological marvels of the coming decades, we can ensure that the values we cherish are maintained in the face of inevitable change, and that the quality of life on this island is as good or better than it is today.

May future generations say of us here today that we were bold and visionary at the turn of the millennium; that we grasped Hawaii's destiny in the global community and produced a quality of life unparalleled in the world; and that as we led Hawaii through a period of unprecedented change, we never allowed our island values to be compromised.

Let them say that we met the challenges of our time and that our stewardship marked the renaissance of Honolulu.